Excite... *on the ground—* *and in the Air!*

Omar and Olympus were in their copter chasing after Jake and Wilson in their Duster.

"We attack!" thundered Olympus.

Omar brought the copter up, then swooped down. Its blades cut off the tip of the Duster's wing.

"They're trying to kill us!" cried Wilson.

Down came the copter and chopped off the Duster's tail. Another pass from the copter. Their under-carriage was sliced away. It sailed off and split into sections.

"They're forcing us down!" cried Wilson.

Jake flew straight at a suspension bridge. The copter rose above the bridge and the Duster flew under it.

"That does it!" cried Olympus. "Buzz them one more time, Omar! *Everybody open fire!*"

The Cat From Outer Space

by
Ted Key

PUBLISHED BY POCKET BOOKS NEW YORK

Another *Original* publication of POCKET BOOKS

POCKET BOOKS, a Simon & Schuster division of
GULF & WESTERN CORPORATION
1230 Avenue of the Americas, New York, N.Y. 10020

ISBN: 0-671-81740-X

First Pocket Books printing June, 1978

2nd printing

Trademarks registered in the United States and other countries.

Printed in the U.S.A.

For Anne

Chapter One

With staccato, rapid-fire precision, the teletype machine printed, "PHX — X E40 BKU 0 — 0 OVC 11 2 208/54/51/060/015. . . ."

It was supplying weather information for the Western Sector Air Defense Radar Station near San Ramon. The town itself was actually six and a half miles to the southwest. A cluster of dilapidated dwellings, several shops and bars, it served as a haven for the Air Force personnel who manned the desert base twenty-four hours a day.

The extremities of weather had left their mark on the radar station. Not three years old, the metal shacks were stained and scorched, presenting a deceiving picture indeed, for the base was an essential link in the defense system of North America.

Now it was late fall, 8:17 in the evening. The still air was crisp and cold. Overhead lay an infinite black sky. Mists of stars bore testimony to ancient galaxies. Other lands. Other life.

". . . Roger, have him i-dent," said Sergeant

Dessik. He was huddled over a computerized radarscope.

The small air-conditioned room was obviously not designed for men, but for their equipment. Five Air Force enlisted men were hunched over the methodic machines. Each scope scanned a sector. Low voices, speaking casually, reflected the monotony. It was a dull, routine evening.

Into the mouthpiece of his headset, Sergeant Lyman was saying, ". . . Los Angeles Center Air Defense Command reference two seven three. L.A., will you please confirm that as Flight Twenty-seven? Miami to Los Angeles?"

In the background could be heard the low voices of other operators, ". . . tracking zero nine zero. . . . Roger, sector two. . . . He's appearing to be doing two fifty . . ."

"Okay, Los Angeles," said Sergeant Lyman. "Just wanted to be sure—he seems to be three point seven knots off course. . . ."

A blip whipped across his scope, cut a sharp ninety-degree turn, and shot off the screen. Lyman froze. He was speechless.

"Jeepers," he finally managed. "You see that, Dessik?"

"See what?"

The blip reappeared. It caromed off from the side and raced across the screen and disappeared. Dessik had caught a glimpse of it. Lyman pressed a button. In the window of his computer was a printout of range, bearing, altitude. . . .

"That's *impossible!*" said Sergeant Lyman. Sergeant Dessik leaned over for a reading. He wore a stunned expression.

"Brother!" he cried. "There's got to be a malfunction!"

As he spoke, the blip reappeared. It made two abrupt ninety-degree passes and whirled off the screen The men stared at each other. Lyman pressed for another reading, confirmed his worst fears, then seized a hot-line telephone. Dessik stared incredulously at the scope.

"Lieutenant?" Lyman said into the phone. "Sergeant Lyman. Something very unusual, sir."

Lieutenant Arnold Bliss had his feet on the desk when the phone buzzed. He had been reading a magazine in the adjacent room. Bliss was no more than twenty-five years old, a somewhat arch, slightly built man with a permanent five-o'clock shadow which he found appealing. It confirmed his macho image of himself. The officer's radar, with computer tie-in and a repeater, befitted his station- -that of command function. Someone must have had great faith in his ability, because he had the authority to send out planes to intercept bogies.

"What?!" cried Lieutenant Bliss. His feet came off the desk "It did *what?!*"

"Bearing zero nine zero, range one two zero, altitude ninety-one miles," added Lyman.

"Come off it, Lyman, *ninety-one* miles?" Bliss began making notes. "You sure it's not a second-stage rocket, a worn-out weather satellite . . . some kind of space garbage?"

"Space garbage, sir?" said Lyman. "Moving at Mach two eight?"

"Mach two eight? That's twenty-one thousand miles an hour!"

"Yes, sir. Heading two seven zero. Oh, and one thing more, sir. It makes ninety-degree turns."

Lyman had hardly finished when the door to the duty officer's room popped open. Lieutenant Bliss strode swiftly to Sergeant Lyman's scope.

"Now that's impossible . . ." he was saying, then stopped. On Lyman's scope, a blip had just maneuvered a ninety-degree turn. It reversed itself, made two abrupt ninety-degree maneuvers, then, almost as a topper, displayed a one-hundred-thirty-five-degree cutback. Lieutenant Bliss may have appeared to lack maturity, but he didn't lack intelligence. He grabbed the red hot-line telephone and was instantly connected with his commanding officer.

"Major, Lieutenant Bliss," he began. "I'm sorry, sir, I didn't mean to interrupt your dinner, but something's come up. What, sir? Well, sir, we've got a blip, sir. Yes, I know that's not unusual, but this blip moves at Mach two eight and makes ninety-degree turns."

The major's reply was garbled, but Bliss seemed to make sense of it.

5

"No, sir, I'm not, sir," he said. "I *never* drink, sir, not even *off* duty."

The object of his concern was, as of that moment, almost ninety-three miles above San Ramon's large fiber-glass, white geodesic dome, which housed the radar antenna. The odd-shaped spaceship sailed silently in a field of stars, reflecting, on its metallic underside, a pale shadow of the distant blue-green earth.

The craft was truly a metallic wonder. From a distance, it was a vision of serenity, benign. Yet on closer examination there were suggestions of malevolence. From its bulging hull several protruding, bulbous "eyes" circled its midsection. Offshoots of sparse, wiry whiskers, obviously antennae, cropped out fore and aft. A warm, iridescent radiance suffused the strange object, and from an interior source came a low, repetitive hum. One would have to be within a few feet of the ship to hear it. The body of the craft was not small, not overbearing, yet the dynamics of its strange design were far from reassuring. In fact, they were menacing.

Someone aboard was in electronic communication with someone, somewhere. The sounds were low, sometimes nasal, often suggestive of muffled howls almost catlike in intonation.

"This is Zunar Five Jay calling Mother Ship," said the voice. "Hello, Mother. Come in, Mother. This is Zunar Five Jay. Adjusting temperature controls."

"Zunar Five Jay, this is Mother. Continue Exercise Earthsearch, align coaxial." The reply had a canned effect, as if coming through a loudspeaker.

"Coaxial aligned."

"Read, please," said the voice from the Mother Ship.

"Reading, Maxon level falling to zone three, gerd rate steady at . . ."

A wailing alarm bell was heard. It rose in crescendo, then fell, over and over. The voices took on a strident urgency. Some sort of crisis.

"Traject, traject, Zunar!" howled the Mother Ship. "Coming at you from quadrant three zero!"

"I see it, Mother!" was the reply.

"Curtail power!" came the instructions.

"Complying!"

Out of the impenetrable darkness loomed a section of a manmade rocket, hurling toward the spaceship. Almost as in slow motion, it caromed off the top of the ship's hull and whined out of sight. The craft was hurt. It fluttered erratically, as if to stabilize itself. Even its hue suggested mechanical failure. Short bolts of lightning—yellows, greens, reds—whipped from the hull. Once radiant, the craft's luster began to pale, then to fade. Wounded, it couldn't hold its course. Gone was the reassuring, steady hum. An eerie, reverberating whine split the ear, over which could be heard the clatter of some sort of computer. The alarm bell stopped ringing.

"Power short, Mother!" cried the voice from the ship. "Feels like a ten twenty! Stabilizer failing!"

"Have you in viewer, four eight. Thrust negative."

"Give me a printout, please," came from the spacecraft.

There was silence as the ship began to lose altitude. Then, as if from a canned electronic instrument, came the muffled rat-a-tat of a distant computer. It held for a moment, then ceased.

"Station Red," instructed the Mother Ship. "Set gauges. No time for space repair. You're heading for a soft landing, Zunar Five Jay."

"Read, Mother. Any numbers?"

The craft began an erratic descent toward earth. Again the clatter of the Mother Ship's computer, over which could be heard a voice from the mother ship. The tone was distinctly catlike.

"Numbers coming. Stand by."

"Imprinting," came from the spaceship.

The orders came in the tone of a command. "After landing, make necessary repairs and launch to rendezvous with us at grid dissect eight three zero four. Set digital clonometer . . . *now!*"

The clatter of the computer stopped.

"Clonometer set."

"We'll make contact at six nine hours minus twelve," said the Mother Ship.

The reply had a note of concern. "That's all?

8

I mean, six nine minus twelve is an awfully tight squeeze, Mother."

"Unavoidable, Zunar. Our capability is for just one orbit correction before mission termination."

There was no immediate reply to this. Finally, "And . . . if I can't make the launch time?"

"The next mission to this galaxy is due in one one five," said the mother ship.

"Days?"

"Years. Good luck, Zunar Five Jay. Over and out."

From the spaceship came a toneless, "So long, Mother."

The earth filled the sky and the spaceship plunged toward it.

Chapter Two

The farmer and his wife were sleeping peacefully in their bed when the dog, lying at their feet, began to whimper. The farmer stretched his arm and managed to rub the dog's head.

"Bad dream, fella?" mumbled the farmer.

The whimpering continued. A strange green, ethereal light flicked on and off in the room, beamed in from the window. The farmer opened his eyes but said nothing. From somewhere in the distance he could hear the cackling of startled chickens. Ducks were quacking. Above the sounds of frightened farm animals he heard a puzzling, distant, repetitive hum. He rose and moved swiftly to the window. His wife stirred as he cautiously raised the blind. She turned toward him apprehensively.

"What is it?" she said.

"Real weird," said the farmer.

Through the window, he looked out on a night mist. It drifted among the sheds, the barn, and the sloping fields. Pigs were scampering in their pen. Goats, fowl, and horses were reacting in fright. A pulsating green light emanated from beyond a shrubbed hill, almost orchestrated by the low, unearthly, repetitive sound.

"Over the hill somewhere," managed the farmer.

His wife edged toward the window as the farmer searched for his clothes. They were draped over a chair. He dressed hastily in the dark as his wife stared incredulously through the window.

"What's got into 'em? What's that light?" she whispered.

Her husband was almost dressed now. He reached into a closet for a rifle.

"Don't move from this room, hon," said the farmer. To the dog he said, "Come on, Dutch."

The dog was off the bed and lying near the far wall. He was trembling.

The farmer's wife said, "Watch yerself, Jim."

"You coming, boy?" the farmer said to the dog.

The animal whimpered and didn't budge.

"Suit yourself," said the farmer, and left, clutching the rifle.

He was still tucking in his shirt as he strode from the house. Caught in the eerie, pulsating light, he stopped. Then he moved swiftly beyond the frightened farm animals and toward the hill. The glow became intense and the repetitive sound reached an ear-splitting pitch. The farmer cautiously began to slow down as he approached the crest of the hill. Bushes obscured his vision. Fright gripped him. Something crazy was going on and he didn't like it. He began to crawl, groveling from one shrub to another. He reached the top of the hill and stared down into a cove. His eyes opened in horror.

Tucked in a hollow no more than a hundred yards away was a monstrous metallic creature. It was resting on four long, crouching, skeletal supports. Blinking amber eyes, almond shaped, revolved under a protruding circular brow. Coming from somewhere in the bowels of the object was an ominous howl. The ship, pulsating as if it were alive, had assumed the protective coloring of its environment—green.

The farmer gasped, then slithered backward down the hill. When he felt he could rise with impunity, he scrambled terror-stricken toward the farmhouse.

A section of the craft's fuselage began to whine and whirl, creating an amorphous exit. Out of the ship's gloomy interior stepped a cat. He studied the surroundings curiously, peering right, then left, then down, twelve feet toward the ground. He made no sound. Then he sat on his haunches and thought. Around his neck was a collar studded with scintillating colored crystals.

In the farmhouse, an almost hysterical farmer was phoning the sheriff. A wide-eyed wife clutched his one free hand while the dog, Dutch, whimpered in a corner.

"Right. Right," the sheriff told him. He took

notes. "Yeah, sure does. You and Lil just stay in the house and lock the doors, Jim. We'll be right over."

He hung up, yelled for his deputy, and was almost out of his office when the thought occurred to him. It might be wise to have a little backup. If this thing was as crazy as it sounded, he might need it. He phoned the state police.

It was all true. Jim's description was all too accurate. And frightening. The craft had not budged. No life could be seen. But the sound, almost as if fingernails were being scratched against a blackboard, set the nerves on end. The pulsating light cast a haunting green sweep across three frightened faces peering over the hill. The sheriff, his deputy, and the state patrol officer had seen enough. They scrambled down the hill, gasping in terror. This was not a local law enforcement problem. Where did you start with a thing like this? Who the devil knew what it was, or what it might do? Not for them, no, sir. They weren't messing around. This called for the feds, and not their law enforcement agencies either. The *big* boys.

Within an hour and a half, General Cornwallis Stilton was on the scene. It was an assignment not given to him by chance.

A three-starred Air Force general who thrived on danger, General Cornwallis Stilton was a commanding physical presence. Not just his ramrod posture. His intimidating voice was strident, rapid, and authoritative. Over the years, the general had witnessed the motion picture *Patton* eighteen times and, by osmosis, had absorbed the mystique of the dazzling strategist. Stilton carried no pearl-handled revolvers, to be sure, but he was never without a riding crop. The snapping crack of leather against the general's thighs often under-scored his orders. That he slept with the whip, however, was a rumor with no basis in fact.

The general arrived at the farm in a convoy consisting of two armed jeeps, two weapons car-riers, and his own command car. Riding with the general in the four-door sedan were Colonel Woodruff, Captain Anderson, and Sergeant Duffy. They were aides who had been selected by the general personally—not for their size or strength or wisdom, but for their military de-meanor. To him, they represented the epitome in the Military Man. They were stalwart, obedient, apt, and attentive. Of the three soldiers, only one had a reasonably responsive brain—Sergeant Duffy—and quite often he made use of it. This was fortunate because the one good brain had to serve the three of them. But this was of no interest to the general, who was concerned only with action and knee-jerk response.

General Stilton, his large, dark sunglasses wrapped around a self-righteous face, led all three aides to the top of the hill, where he im-mediately exposed himself to possible line of fire. If he registered fright at the strange object that he saw in his binoculars, he did not display it. Only Sergeant Duffy had sense enough to be scared.

"Don't see any hammer and sickle, do you, Woodruff?" the general said finally.

"It might be on the inside, General," Colonel Woodruff replied.

The general ignored him. "No sign of life, either. Get me the Pentagon, Colonel. Red priority. I want to speak to the chiefs."

Colonel Woodruff lowered his binoculars and bellowed, "Captain!"

Captain Anderson's aide did all the work. "Ser---geant!" cried the captain.

Sergeant Duffy flicked on his walkie-talkie and said softly, "Sequoia here, come in, Rover. . . ."

None of the men bothered to glance at the ground. If they had, they would have seen, sitting directly behind the general's right boot, a cat, a strikingly beautiful animal who was wearing a collar of jeweled crystals. His head was cocked as he peered up at the soldiers, still absorbed with the spaceship.

Three hours later a skycrane helicopter was hovering over the spacecraft and the scene had become one of frenzied activity. Floodlights cast a bright light on the army engineers who were hooking up the vehicle to a fluttering helicopter. Some men kept a respectful distance from the craft, for though its howl was now subdued, the squinting, piercing "eyes" were still active. Were they deadly lasers? Were they radioactive? One could never be too certain.

Several hundred feet beyond, flanked by his aides, General Stilton was confronting the farmer, his wife, the sheriff, his deputy, and the state trooper. He was laying down the law.

"Wipe it out of your minds! You understand? You have seen nothing and heard nothing!"

"Yes, sir," said the farmer, weakly.

"We'll want them for debriefing. Take their names, Colonel." The general did an abrupt about-face and strode up toward his command position. It was a floodlit boulder on top of a hill.

"Captain!" cried the colonel, and followed his superior.

"Ser---geant!" bellowed the captain and moved after the colonel. Sergeant Duffy withdrew a pad and a pencil, licked the lead point, then began asking for names, addresses, and phone numbers.

Men scurried clear of the spacecraft. The engineer in charge of field operations tested wires, bolts, and connections, then checked again. He had been assigned to General Stilton once before and remembered. This officer brooked no error. Satisfied, the engineer stepped aside and shouted toward the hill.

"Whenever you are, General!"

A mighty Caesar surveying his legions, General Stilton pompously raised his riding crop. His stiff legs were spread wide. Decision. Action.

"To Hopscotch!" thundered the general.

The riding crop cracked a thigh. The helicopter rose slowly into the air, lifting its eerie cargo, now swinging slightly off kilter. The howl had begun to fade, but the "eyes" continued to circle as the helicopter and its cargo vanished into the night.

The general cracked his whip again. Job well done. Swiftly, he made an about-face and strode toward his command car. The aides moved to follow, each in his proper place, a slight step to the right and one step back of his superior.

Sergeant Duffy brought up the rear. One step behind him, slightly to his right, walking in perfect tandem with the four soldiers, was the cat. He was unobserved.

The sergeant rushed forward. With proper salutes, he opened the rear door for his general and colonel. They stepped into the car, sat, and the door was closed. The sergeant saluted, stepped forward, and opened the front door of the car on the passenger side. More salutes. Captain Anderson took his proper place, made a salute, and it was returned.

Now Sergeant Duffy briskly stepped toward the driver's side of the sedan. The cat followed him, but stopped to look up at the back trunk. The crystals in his collar began to warm, then glow intensely, the violet evolving to deep blue to turquoise to chartreuse to yellow and orange and finally to a deep, sparkling vermillion. The lid of the trunk lifted open, the cat hopped into the luggage compartment, and the lid flapped shut. The command car pulled away with a roar.

Chapter Three

Hopscotch was the code name for a mothballed, lighter-than-air airfield, uniquely isolated. It had been used infrequently since World War II, but from time to time blimps and experimental dirigibles were tested and housed on its grounds. There had been some Defense Department talk of using helium craft for heavy military cargo—not now, of course, but sometime in the future. And in any case, who really knew. Weapons were never declared obsolete in the Defense Department, merely pigeon-holed. So the field was kept open and fully staffed. Suppose Russia decided to go in for blimps? Hopscotch was well guarded.

A distant light faintly illuminated the three cars parked outside the small hangar. One was the general's command car. Two others were marked NASA.

Two soldiers, accompanied by fierce patrol dogs, moved inside a cyclone fence topped with electric barbed wire. In bold letters, a sign read:

U.S. AIRFIELD, TRESPASSERS WILL BE PROSE-
CUTED.

In the far corner of the field were barracks
and tin-plated buildings. The silhouettes of tanks
and weapons carriers could be seen in the distance.

But no one from this base was admitted to
the hangar this night. Only experts. By invita-
tion. With clearance. This had been General
Stilton's specific order. His aides stood a respectful distance behind him as he conferred
with one of NASA's experts, twenty yards to the
right of the object of interest.

Two scientists from NASA, wearing white
jackets, white slippers, and white gloves, moved
gingerly inside the spaceship, cautiously testing
features of the craft with metered instruments.
High above all this, secure in the rafters, rested
a cat.

He observed without displaying emotion or
alarm. In fact, he was rather a patient creature,
slender and assured, whose fur was short and
whose colorings resembled those of the Abyssin-
ian breed. As a pet, he would have been nice
to fondle.

The spaceship had been placed directly in the
hangar's center. It had taken on the coloration
of the hangar's interior—dull orange—obviously
some sort of defensive mechanism. Now the "eyes"
barely circled and the "sound" was muted.

The two NASA technologists examined the

console of the spacecraft. The instruments, it seemed, were at a very low eye level and manual dexterity appeared to be necessary for their operation. There were no levers, buttons, or switches, and no chairs as such—only protuberances that broke up from the floor, for what purpose was anybody's guess.

"Amazing," said the first scientist. "It uses adaptive coloration."

"The big question is, where does it get its propulsion?" asked his colleague.

"Beats me. But if I had to take bets . . ."

He nodded toward an oval-shaped piece of equipment. Whether it was metal or plastic was difficult to judge, but it *was* shaped like an artichoke and appeared to emit an inner source of light. In fact, a four-inch rainbow aura enveloped the sharp-edged leaves. The size of a man's hand, this "artichoke" turned ever so slowly in space, unattached, in a transparent box three feet above the base of the cabin. No wires, cells, or transistors were attached to it. Nothing, in fact.

The phenomenon intrigued the two men. One ran an instrument over it.

"No reaction," he said.

Below, several yards away, General Stilton was listening intently. An administrator from NASA was saying, "Unquestionably. A brilliant technological achievement, General. There is nothing like it in the state of the art."

"You trying to tell me something, Allison?" the general said.

"It's definitely not one of ours, General."

"How about Russia?" asked Stilton.

"Certainly not Russia. It's far beyond the capability of any nation on . . ."

He was interrupted. The general had had enough pussyfooting.

"Okay, Allison, lay it on the line. Whose is it?"

The NASA chief studied the officer. "I don't know," he said.

The general roared, "Well, we'd better find out, believe you me! Double pronto! Because if *you* don't know where that thing came from, and *I* don't know where it came from, this country's in trouble! Big, big trouble!"

"Yes, sir."

"Not manmade, he says! What's that leave us? *Outer space!*"

Allison nodded. "With no sign of the pilot."

"Big, big trouble!" cried the general. "While you and I are talking, gentlemen—*this very minute*—some slimy, green-headed, twelve-legged creep could be crawling into the White House!"

High in the rafters, the cat rose. He yawned, then stretched, then lay down again to await developments.

Suddenly, the sound from the spaceship ceased. The "eyes" blinked off, then stopped orbiting. To the startled gathering the patina of the ship

grew from a dull orange to its natural color—
burnished silver.

The general's mouth was agape. "What's going
on up there?" he bellowed.

The two NASA scientists stepped out of the
cabin and peered down in triumph. One held
a three-foot-long pair of laboratory prongs which
grasped the transparent box. Dead center, the
"artichoke" was spinning slowly.

"We have it, General!" he cried.

"Definitely the energy source!" his colleague
asserted.

"That tiny thing?" cried the general.

"No question," was the reply.

The general strode up to the ship and arched
his head back for a clearer view. "Lord help us,"
he was heard to mutter. Then he turned, arched
his shoulders, and addressed the assemblage.

"With that kind of know-how, they'll be dust-
ing us off Cloud Nine!"

Colonel Woodruff said, "Gentlemen, . . ." but
the general interrupted.

"This could well be the gravest crisis in our
nation's history!" cried Stilton.

Allison said, "In my opinion . . ."

"No opinions!" cried the general. "This is no
tinker toy we're playing with, gentlemen, believe you me! We're in kindergarten compared
to this capability!"

"I agree," the colonel nodded.

"And running out of time!" Stilton cracked

the crop. "I want to know who made that thing, who flew it, and where it came from! Not tomorrow! Double pronto! *Now!*"

"We'll get our best minds down here, General," said the NASA chief.

"You bet your sweet life you will! Your best minds and our best minds and the fattest I.Q.'s in the nation—we're getting our tail out of the wringer! Woodruff!"

"Yes, sir!"

"Get Hungerford at Air!" ordered the general. "Call Steinmetz at Hopkins! Lasser, Billings, and Cranhammer—get them Harvards off their tennis courts!"

"Yes, *sir!*"

"We're up against genius, gentlemen! We'd better come up with some genius of our own!"

Chapter Four

The acronym ERL was etched in a huge concrete slab sitting bolt upright on the lawn. It greeted all who approached the main gateway to the grounds of the Energy Resources Laboratory reserve. Behind a vine-covered, highly secured fence, which stretched through the eucalyptus, lay at least a dozen look-alike brick buildings. Some were three stories high, some only two, but all were massive.

They lay among beautifully manicured grounds with circling, intertwining roads and walkways leading to a spacious parking lot. Government money well spent.

Well spent or not, it bore testament to the orderly, didactic mind of the director of operations, Doctor Leopold Heffel. He was a tall, humorless, ingratiating, and quite impatient man of about fifty. And today would not be one of his better days. Today he was meeting with General Stilton.

And his aides. And the convoy that accompanied the command car to ERL shortly after the sun broke. Soldiers armed with automatic weapons planted themselves inside and outside the administration building.

What had happened, it seemed, was that Heffel had been aroused out of a sound sleep at three in the morning. For a man who could not function without the usual eight hours, this was discomfiting. The voice he heard was Stilton's. It was a commanding voice, a voice to be obeyed. It spoke in the name of the Joint Chiefs, National Security, and the White House. Heffel's best brains would be in a secured ERL conference room no later than 0700 that morning. No later. His keenest, sharpest people. No questions asked. A matter of *highest* priority.

Heffel made the necessary phone calls, then brewed coffee for himself and thought. What was *that* all about? Well, the night was shot. He couldn't go back to sleep. He shaved, showered, and drove off in his car.

At 0700 exactly, he and ten of his finest minds flanked a long table in the administration building. A bolted, double-locked steel box rested directly in front of the general, who stood at the table's head buttressed by his aides. Taking it all in from a ledge outside the window was a cat.

Doctor Heffel made the introductions. "Doctor Robeson of Cal Tech, General," he said. "Our expert in fossil fuel. Professor Hurakawa of Johns

Hopkins. Doctor Elizabeth Bartlett, who heads thermal . . ."

The woman, in her mid-twenties, was considered a comer in scientific circles. She nodded, but received no response from the general. But then, it was hard to tell what really went on behind the general's sunglasses. The fact that Bartlett was beautiful, young, and well proportioned made no apparent impression on the officer. But who knew? Stilton was hard-nosed, and one-tracked. Perhaps he was only thinking, "No diversions today." But *other* days?

"And over here," added Doctor Heffel. "Doctor Carl Link, who's doing some inspiring research in garbage . . ."

He turned toward Link. Or where the man had been standing. Link was at the far end of the room, speaking on the phone in a low, husky voice.

"Doctor Link!" cried Heffel.

"Only a second, Doctor Heffel," said Link. "Relaying classified information to a colleague."

Doctor Link was a tall, laconic man in his late thirties whose pleasant face seemed to mask an imaginative mind. He turned his back to the others and cupped the mouthpiece.

"Right, Ernie," he almost whispered. "The Lakers by a point and a half. When will you have the line on the Knicks and Philly?"

". . . and Professor Debney, who's into ocean movement . . ." continued Doctor Heffel.

The cat moved stealthily along the ledge and hopped onto an adjoining window. It fronted on the washroom adjoining the conference room. On the cat's neck, the collar began to warm, then gleam. The window slid up noiselessly. The creature dropped onto the washroom floor as the window shut without sound.

Now he stared up at a doorknob. He could hear ERL's chief of operations in the adjoining room. The door between the washroom and the conference room opened and the cat entered. Not a soul witnessed this. Instinctively, the animal selected the most comfortable resting place, a cushion on a leather sofa, then tilted one ear toward the conversation.

"Doctor Keystone, who heads Nu-clear, and over here, Mister Rupert Stallwood, who heads up procurement and supplies . . ." Doctor Heffel did a double take. "What are *you* doing here, Stallwood?!"

"Just thought you could use my services, sir," said Stallwood, all teeth and smiles. "When the call went out for the emergency meeting, I felt it incumbent—"

"You seem to have that habit, Stallwood. And I'm getting tired of it. Scientists with a triple clearance only. *Out.*"

"If I may say so, sir—" his spirit was never dampened—"we in administration—"

"Stallwood!"

"—might well serve as a balance to you technologists in the theoretical arena. What I have to contribute—and I'll put it to you frankly, sir—is genuine, old-fashioned—"

"Stallwood!"

"Horse sense."

"Stallwood!" said Heffel disdainfully. "When I need our pencils sharpened, I'll call on you!"

"And sharp I shall make them, sir!"

"Out!"

Heffel thrust the man through the door and shut it fast. The door opened. Stallwood again.

"Sir . . ."

Heffel slammed the door.

A nauseatingly cheerful man through all his waking hours, Rupert Stallwood was an easy man to dislike. Not only because he was a phony, but because he was an irrepressible bustler who was forever poking his nose in other people's business. What made matters worse, he was a fastidious, immaculate fop. And a whistler. Never on key.

Stallwood adjusted his tie, beamed a cheerful good morning to the two soldiers standing guard at the door, and, whistling Dixie, off key, stepped briskly down the corridor.

Doctor Heffel returned to the table. "My apologies, General. Now where was I? Oh, yes, over here is Professor . . ."

"That's it, Doctor!" barked the general. "Enough! I'm not here for a roll call!"

"Yes, sir. I was just trying to . . ."

"I'm here for some brain picking!" The general slapped his crop against his knee. "We're wasting time, Heffel!"

"Of course, General. Everyone's attention, please! Doctor Link?"

"That's it, Professor," Link said on the phone. "I'll call tomorrow with more input. Goodbye." He hung up and joined the others.

"You ready, Doctor?" the general sarcastically inquired of Heffel.

"Anytime you say, sir."

"Colonel!" barked the general.

"Captain!" cried the colonel.

"Ser---geant!!" bellowed the captain.

Sergeant Duffy slid the mysterious box forward. With a series of keys he began to unlock it.

"What you are about to see, ladies and gentleman, is top secret!" cried the general. "The United States Government will countenance no leaks!"

The sergeant raised the box above the center of the table and turned the box upside down. Ever so carefully, he opened the lid, then lifted the box up and away, free and clear of its contents. There was the "artichoke." Without visible support, ever so slowly, a foot above the table, it floated. It made no sound. A rainbow aura surrounded it. The scientists reacted in astonishment. Instinctively, some drew back from the table.

The first to recover was Doctor Heffel.

"What's holding it up?"

"Nothing!" barked General Stilton. He slashed the air above and below the "artichoke" with his crop.

"Amazing," uttered Heffel.

"Where'd you get it?" asked one expert.

"What is it?" inquired another.

"A propulsion unit of some sort, ladies and gentlemen. Never mind where we got it," the general said. "We have other experts working on that. What we want to know from you is, *what makes it run?*"

No one replied. The scientists stared at the object as if transfixed.

"Nobody has a hypothesis?" asked the general.

Someone ventured, "The energy source could be atomic."

"We've checked on that. Negative!" said the general. Some of the scientists stepped closer to the object but others held a respectful distance.

Liz Bartlett said, "Could it be direct conversion, utilizing thermionic emission . . . ?"

"Checked out! Negative!" cried the general. He turned to Link.

The general appeared to be consulting him. Link shrugged. "It's not propelled by *garbage,* General."

The cat watched intently. Not a purr out of him.

In the corridor, Rupert Stallwood made another pass at reentry. "Quite a bit of hush-hush going on in there," he said airily to the soldiers guarding the door. No response. They stared straight ahead, firmly clasping their automatic weapons.

Stallwood moved toward the door. The reaction was immediate. Both weapons whipped to instant ready.

"Excellent! Very good, men! Just a test!" said Stallwood brightly. "This country is in good hands, believe you me! Carry on!" And he strode down the hall. He ducked into the first hallway, furtively glanced around, then popped into a phone booth.

He deposited a coin in the box and cradled the receiver on his shoulder. But instead of dialing he withdrew a cigarette lighter from his pocket. From inside his jacket he took a metal pencil, telescoped it into a foot-long antenna, and screwed it into the lighter. Then he opened a flap which revealed a miniature microphone, plugged in an earpiece, and pressed a switch. There was a buzz. Stallwood whispered into the lighter.

"Jellyfish calling Olympus. Jellyfish calling Olympus. Come in, Olympus . . . hello? . . . May I speak directly to Mister Olympus, please? . . . Of *course* it's urgent, you don't think I'd. . . . yes . . . yes . . . very . . . thank you. . . ."

He paused, then slipped a cigarette into his mouth, flicked the lighter, and lit up.

"Mister Olympus? Jellyfish, sir." He capped the flame on the lighter. The lid sprang back. The lighter was still burning. "I think I'm onto something *very hot*, sir." Down came the cap of the lighter. It sprang back. The flame was even higher. "Very hot, sir . . . *Jellyfish* . . . *Jellyfish!* . . . your man at ERL! . . ." Every effort to douse the flame failed. It was now six inches high. "Jellyfish—j-e-l-l . . ." The flame would not go out. He stepped on the lighter. No luck. Now bent over, "I think I'm onto something very . . . Sir, are you . . ." In desperation he smothered the flames with his hands. "Yaaaaaahhhhhhhhh!!" he wailed. "Oh, not *you*, sir, I was just . . . oh, I wouldn't, sir, don't hang up . . . sir . . . when you hear what I have to tell you . . . sir? . . . sir . . . oh, much more interesting than my last report, sir . . ." Olympus was outraged about something. Stallwood pulled the lighter back.

"Well, isn't that a matter of opinion, sir?" continued Stallwood. "I still maintain that the amount of paper shredded weekly in an installation of this size could well give us the statistical insight into . . ." He was cut short. "Yes, sir, consider it dropped, sir." His hoarse voice sank as he spoke with greatest confidentiality. "Well, sir, I think this is going to interest you. Right this *minute*, Doctor Heffel's in a secret meeting with a three-star general and our most brilliant scientists. . . . What are they meeting about? I don't know what they're meeting about, sir, it's a secret." There was an angry blast from Olympus. "Find out? Sir, they've got armed guards with guns and . . . but, sir, I don't think there's any way I can get back into that . . ." The torrent of abuse stopped him, but only momentarily. "Yes, sir. I will, sir, I'll get in. Right away. Immediately if not sooner, sir!"

Back in the conference room the scientists had made no headway and one was still expounding.

". . . might very likely rest with the oscillatory motion principle . . . that is, in the static magnetic field. . . ."

What could be seen of the general's face was grim. He had just about had it.

"Negative!" he barked.

A knock on the door. Heffel flung it open and there was ingratiating Stallwood.

"What?" cried Heffel. Stallwood tried to peek into the room.

"Just checking, sir. Need anyone to take notes? My shorthand is . . ."

"No!"

"How about some coffee? Tea? Milk? A diet root beer?"

"Out!" screamed Heffel, and slammed the door in Stallwood's face. "The man's impossible!"

Stilton rapped the table hard with his crop.

"Do any of you—*any*—have a solid evaluation? Not a *guess*—I can do my own guessing— a solid *premise*? Do you?" The general glanced around the room. "Well?"

Elizabeth Bartlett cleared her throat.

"Do you think it would be fruitful to bring Doctor Wilson into this discussion, Doctor Heffel?" she said.

That was the last straw for Heffel. "Wilson!"

"He might well have an applicable theory," she said.

"Ridiculous! The man's completely disorganized!" cried Heffel.

"Who are you talking about?" asked General Stilton.

"Doctor Wilson, sir. He's in my car pool. We live in the same building," she added.

"That certainly qualifies him," snapped the general. There was appreciative laughter from his aides.

Elizabeth said, "He happens to be a brilliant young physicist, sir. A recent loan from Cal Tech."

"A bad loan, General," said Heffel. "Bearing absolutely no interest." Elizabeth didn't find this amusing but *his* colleagues did.

She said, "I grant you he's unorthodox. But most theorists are. The man has a long list of achievements, General. I've read his papers and I've found them to be . . ."

"Doctor Bartlett," interrupted her superior. "General Stilton isn't interested in . . ."

"Get Wilson!" barked Stilton.

"What?" said Doctor Heffel.

"Get him! What he has to say can't be any worse than what I've heard so far!"

"Yes, sir," said Heffel weakly, and glared at Elizabeth. She chose to ignore him. Heffel stepped to the door and opened it. There was Stallwood.

"A Danish, sir?"

"No Danish! Guards!" An ERL security guard stood at attention across the hall. "Hoffman, get Doctor Wilson up here. *Now*." The guard hurried off and Heffel slammed the door in Stallwood's beaming face.

Elizabeth ignored Heffel's hostility as he returned to the table. She said, "I don't think you're going to be disappointed, General."

In his basement laboratory, Doctor Frank Wilson was in deep contemplation. He appeared to be studying one of the many complex mathematical equations scrawled on a blackboard. Obviously, this one was of special importance. He hesitated, reached a decision, then chalked up "Pick up laundry" under the words "Things to do."

And continued to deliberate.

In his late twenties, Wilson was a direct and caring man who many considered to be eccentric. Which he was, but this came about neither by plan or fashion. It was his way. Neither handsome nor plain, his face had a quality of innocence that some women found attractive. His appeal was not to their maternal but their managerial instincts.

Wilson's laboratory was not large. A tiny cubicle, with one small, thin window near the ceiling, it was certainly not a place conducive to creativity.

This might have bothered others, but not Wilson. In fact, in laboratory or home, he was oblivious to his environment. A make-do, egoless soul who neither fumed nor fussed, adaptation rather became him.

As did blackboards. In this lab, they covered not only much of the walls, but a portion of the ceiling, directly over an old misshapen sofa. Lying in that sofa, using a long pointer tipped with chalk, Wilson dreamed up some of his brightest notions.

He rather liked this lab. Pipes crisscrossed overhead. In the far corner was a large mock-up model of the earth's solar system, surrounded by thin slivers of wire, magnetic fields encircling the planets and the sun. The furniture Doctor Heffel had provided were castoffs at best—a table, a desk, a filing cabinet, and a chair with wired supports. Books and notes were scattered about, while to one side model airplanes of vintage type hung from fishlines.

Obviously this was a theorist's laboratory, but there was one strange contrivance in it which never failed to interest visitors. Wilson had built it himself—an intricate machine which prepared the physicist's breakfast on order. This machine flanked one whole side of the room and reached a height of at least six feet. At its head, in a small cage, seated on a treadmill, was a white mouse.

"Good morning, Drexel," Wilson said to the mouse. "Black, one sugar, please."

The physicist pressed a button attached to the

cage. A lever dropped in front of the mouse. It securely held a piece of cheese. This fact was made absolutely clear by a small sign that was attached to it. CHEESE, it stated. The mouse galloped on the treadmill in a vain effort to reach the cheese. This set in motion levers, balls, cogs, wheels, and belts, and lit a bunsen burner, which heated a coil of copper pipes. The end result was a steaming cup of coffee into which fell a lump of sugar.

Wilson pressed another switch. It stopped the treadmill. He took the coffee cup, crossed to a globe of the earth, lifted the top, and reached in for a cookie. He gave a portion of it to the mouse.

"Chocolate chip," said Wilson. "Made them myself."

There was a knock on the door. When Wilson opened it, there stood Hoffman, the security guard.

"Doctor Heffel wants you in the conference room, Doctor Wilson," he said. "On the double."

"Me?" the physicist asked. "You sure he said Wilson?"

In the short time that Wilson had been at ERL, not once had the head man called him in. Or even spoken to him. At least on matters of importance. In fact, only on one occasion had Doctor Heffel even visited his laboratory, and that visit was not official.

Heffel liked to snoop. Wilson had walked into his lab quite early one morning to find Heffel sniffing about. The chief made some nonsensical excuse for being there and the mouse treated Heffel to a hot cup of coffee. The mouse, the machine, and the man baffled Heffel, and from that moment on there were only nods and good mornings in the hallways.

"Better come along, sir," said the security guard.

Wilson took his crumpled suit jacket off a chair and stepped toward the door, then stopped. "My pen . . ." he muttered, and opened a desk drawer. He reached the door, then remembered. "Glasses," he muttered, returned to his desk, and started searching. They were in the OUT box. Only one arm was in its coat sleeve, the right arm in the left sleeve, as he took a final sip of coffee. Extending a cellophane bag to the guard, he said, "Pumpkin seeds?"

"I've sworn off," said the guard.

"The complete protein."

"They're waiting, Doctor."

Wilson turned to the mouse. "Hold the fort, Drexel."

General Stilton was pacing the conference room. While the cat watched, he made a complete lap around the table. He looked up into the face of Doctor Carl Link.

"Garbage!" snorted the general.

Link said, "Don't knock garbage, General. Man's greatest resource."

"Man's greatest resource?" cried Stilton.

"Of course. In constant supply. We should treasure it like diamonds," said Link.

"Ye Gods!" moaned the general.

"But do we? No! We feed it to seagulls. *Seagulls!* Utterly ridiculous, General! Can seagulls heat homes? No, sir! This country could save three hundred million barrels of oil a year just by nationalizing garbage!"

The general shook his head. The man was a lunatic.

In the hall, Stallwood lurked about, awaiting his opportunity. He saw it in the form of Doctor Frank Wilson. As the physicist flashed his identification to the soldiers on duty, Stallwood sidled up to him.

"Doctor Wilson." He smiled.

"Stallwood."

"It's about time they got some real manpower in that room, Wilson. Any notion what they're up to?" sniffed Stallwood.

"Nope."

The door opened and there was Heffel. He jerked Wilson into the room, and as Stallwood made a move to follow two automatic weapons crossed in front of his face. Heffel glared at him.

"Strudel?" asked Stallwood.

The door slammed shut, then opened quickly.

"If he tries to come in again, shoot him!" Heffel instructed. The door closed on Stallwood's nose.

With awed admiration, Wilson stared at the propulsion unit floating serenely above the table. He emitted a short whistle of appreciation as he viewed the "artichoke" from all sides, even the underside.

"Well, Doctor Wilson?" said an impatient general.

Almost to himself, Wilson said, "It's beautiful."

The general said, "Don't you have any other observation?"

"Only that it looks like an artichoke, sir."

Heffel was right, another *crackpot*. "We know it looks like an artichoke, Wilson! What makes it tick?"

Wilson was hardly listening. "Mayonnaise?"

"Negative!" cried the general.

Elizabeth shook her head. Why couldn't the man take himself seriously. He had a habit of saying things like that. At the wrong time in the wrong place.

General Stilton nodded toward Doctor Heffel. "Get the nut out of here!" he seemed to say. Wilson resisted as Heffel escorted him toward the door.

"Wait a minute," said Wilson. "I was only joking, sir. You're looking for a theory, sir. Actually in line with the work I've been doing. I've a hunch it's tapping the primal mainstream, General," said Wilson.

Up went the cat's ears.

"The primal mainstream?" asked the puzzled general. He gestured for Heffel to take his hands off Wilson.

"It's everywhere, General. Only on *different frequencies*. The whole electromagnetic spectrum. Cosmic, gamma, X rays, ultraviolet, visible light, infrared, radio waves. And you know how much we finite human beings can probably tune in to? With our senses? Less than five percent."

The cat reacted with a fervent meow.

"The universe makes its own energy, General. We even make it *ourselves*. Take biofeedback. If I taped terminals to your head, General, your brain could run an electric train," said Wilson.

The general gave him a look that could have withered Mount Rushmore.

"Electric train!" he cried.

"Sorry, sir," said Heffel. "I *did* try to tell you . . ."

"Perhaps an electric train wasn't the most apt illustration," began Wilson.

"Never mind explaining, Wilson," said Heffel, as he pushed him toward the door. "Thank you for your contribution."

The physicist pointed at the "artichoke." "You let me have that for two months, General, and I promise you . . ." The door was open and he was on his way out. The cat scooted directly behind him. The door was shut and both were gone.

"Two months! Is the man out of his mind? I can't afford two *hours!*" bellowed the general.

Chin to chin with ERL's director, he barked, "Heffel!"

"Yes, sir!"

"I want action!"

"Yes, sir!"

Stallwood kept pace with Wilson as he headed for his laboratory. "Buddy to buddy, Wilson, what's really going on in there?"

"Buddy to buddy, Stallwood, I haven't the slightest idea."

Wilson was of little help. Stallwood turned back and the physicist moved along the corridor and down two sets of stairs. The cat followed.

Two hands seized the animal. They belonged to Hoffman, the security guard.

"Sorry, fella. No one's allowed in here without a badge," he said to the cat. "You're against regulations."

The cat began to squirm.

"Easy, fella, everything's gonna be all right. We'll find you a fancy home in a real nice animal shelter." He stepped into his office.

The guard flipped through the phone book. The cat took stock of his surroundings. Well-used office equipment, a few lockers and filing cabinets, a desk, and three chairs. On the far side was a window that overlooked lawn and shrubs.

Hoffman found the number. Keeping one hand on the phone book, he tucked the receiver between his neck and shoulders and held the cat firmly. The cat's collar began to glow. The phone leaped off Hoffman's shoulder and shot back to the cradle The guard hesitated. He seemed puzzled. He reached cautiously for the receiver.

The phone crept away. A hand crept after it. The instrument sneaked to the far side of the desk, beyond the guard's reach. Hoffman paused. Wanted to play games, did it? He stood still, then leaped The phone hopped aside.

Hoffman lunged for the instrument. The animal jumped on the window sill. Up went the window and the creature sprang out.

"Hey! Hey, come back here!" cried the guard. He was halfway though the window when it cracked down on his back.

"Yeeeeoooowwwww!" he yelped.

The equation on the blackboard had Wilson stumped Silently, the lab's small window opened to admit the cat. The animal made a soft, noiseless landing, stepped directly behind the physicist, and peered up at the equation.

"Try XY squared over M," he said. His mouth didn't move, but the words could be heard in "catlike" English.

Concentrating intensely, Wilson paid no attention to the voice.

"Won't work," he said. "It's XY *minus* M."

He added this to the equation, moved back to Drexel, and ordered a cup of coffee. "With a touch of cream," he informed the mouse. The machine went into action.

Behind Wilson's back, an eraser rose in the air to wipe out "XY minus M." Up came the chalk to substitute the equation "XY squared over M." The cat's collar was glowing.

"You're with it this morning, Drexel," said Wilson, who slipped the mouse some cheese, then returned to the blackboard with his coffee. He stared at the equation.

"Of course," he finally said. "XY *squared* over M."

The cat meowed. Wilson saw him.

"How'd you get in here?" he asked, then noted the open window. "Oh. You know you're asking for trouble, don't you? Nobody's allowed in here without a triple clearance."

The cat ignored him and circled Wilson's model of the solar system. The magnetic fields of wire looping around the earth seemed to fascinate him.

"The Van Allen belt, Jake," explained Wilson. The cat meowed as if he were aware of the fact.

"Oil and coal's not going to do it. And one of these days that sun of ours is going to turn into a big black hole."

The cat meowed.

"You know where it's really at, Jake?" asked Wilson. The cat peered up at him. "Electromagnetism. We're loaded with it."

The cat's meow was one of agreement.

"Nice to have somebody agree with me for a change."

Stallwood had a sixth sense. He had popped out of his office just in time to see the general and his aides leaving the conference room. Heffel was matching the officer stride for stride. A square box was locked to the colonel's wrist and soldiers clasping automatic machine guns convoyed the group down the corridor.

"I want your best people, full time, Heffel! I'll arrange transportation to Hopscotch!" cried the general.

The colonel stumbled and the box almost hit the floor. The general's face became livid.

"Careful, Colonel!" he shouted.

"Yes, sir!!" said the colonel. The box had not been damaged, thank goodness. The party moved on. But Stallwood's eyes were wide. So *that's* what the excitement was all about—something in that *box*. He scampered into his office and seized a jaunty feathered hat.

"Toothache!" he informed his secretary, and dashed out.

In convoy, General Stilton's command car was just beginning to pull away as Stallwood dashed out of the administration building. He *had* to follow them, but *how?* A motorcycle with sidecar roared up and squealed to a halt. It was marked ENERGY RESOURCES LABORATORY. A messenger dashed up the stairs with a package and had almost reached the door when Stallwood leaped onto the driver's seat. The motor was still running. He waved an open leather identification case at the gaping messenger as his cycle zoomed off in pursuit of the convoy.

"Stallwood! Administration! Emergency!" he bellowed.

The convoy rolled through the secured ERL gate and turned onto the highway. Stallwood was directly behind.

Back in his laboratory, Wilson was petting the cat. He examined the jeweled collar.

"Who owns you, a Greek shipping magnate?" The cat meowed.

"Yeh, I know, you're lonely. Well, you can't hang around here, Jake. Not with Doctor Heffel barging around. He hates animals in his buildings." He stroked the cat's fur. "In fact, he hates *people* in his buildings." Wilson lifted the cat and peered at him nose to nose. "I'll take you home. Just till we find your owner. You won't be lonesome, Jake. My neighbor, Liz—Doctor Bartlett—she has this cat named Lucy Belle. Real cute." He paused. "And the cat's not bad either."

There was a knock on the door and Liz barged in.

"You won't have to drive Professor Link or myself home tonight, Doctor Wilson. Heffel's called a late meeting," she said.

"I don't mind waiting," said Wilson.

"It won't be necessary, Doctor. We've made other arrangements."

"Really no problem," said Wilson.

"*It won't be necessary, Doctor,*" she repeated coolly. Wilson sensed the chill.

"How about some coffee?" he said.

She moved back toward the door. "No thanks."

"Drexel here would be only too happy . . ."

"No thanks, Doctor," she said.

Wilson said, "Chocolate chip cookie?" He barred her from leaving.

"I'm quite busy, Doctor," she said.

"You're mad at something."

"May I leave?"

"Something I did?" he asked.

She studied him. "You really are beyond me."

"Something I *said,*" he asserted.

"You really don't recall, do you, Doctor?" said Elizabeth.

"Recall what?"

"How about *mayonnaise* for a starter," she said.

"Mayonnaise?"

"Or would you prefer *electric trains?*"

"Oh, for heaven's sake, Doctor, is that what's bothering you?" he said.

She'd heard enough. "May I leave, Doctor? I have a very tight schedule."

"I was just joking, Doctor," he said. "Can't a man joke?"

"I didn't hear anybody laughing," she replied. "Especially the general."

The cat meowed. "Has he had water?" Elizabeth asked.

"The general?"

"The *cat!*" said Elizabeth.

"Water?" asked Wilson.

"Cats do get thirsty, you know!" She seized the cat and strode toward a sink. She poured water into a container and placed it on the floor, directly in front of the cat.

Wilson said, "Look, Liz—Doctor Bartlett— just because some general lacks a sense of humor doesn't mean. . . . Look, all I was trying to convey . . ."

"You don't have to make explanations for me, Doctor."

"I want to make explanations for you. Do you know what we were seeing this morning? The magnitude of it? The absolutely mind-boggling magnitude of it?"

Liz stared at him. Her face mellowed. She moved back into the lab and said, "Make it black."

"Make what black?"

"My coffee," she said.

"Your coffee," he said. "Coming right up."

He crossed quickly to the mouse machine and pressed the button. "Black," he instructed Drexel. Liz paid no attention to the familiar contrivance.

"But I don't pretend to understand you, Doctor. A man who can write the paper you did for the *Scientific Quarterly* . . . July twelfth . . . page sixty-three . . ."

Wilson was pleased. "You read it?"

"Of course I read it," she said. "Positively shattering. And then the same man who writes *that* perceptive analysis turns right around—and in the presence of a four-star general . . ."

"Three-star."

". . . some of the country's finest minds . . ."

Wilson placed a cup of coffee in her outstretched hand. "Chocolate chip?" he asked.

"You're not listening." She sipped her coffee.

"I am listening and you're absolutely right. I know it, Liz. I'm my own worst enemy . . ." he added.

"Now don't dramatize it, Frank. I'm only saying that . . ."

"No, no, it's true. It's one of my problems. It always has been. And I intend to do something about it."

She wanted to believe him. "Such as?"

"Believe me," Wilson said.

Her look was kinder. "Okay, Frank," she said softly.

He stared at her. "Look, may I tell *you* something, Liz—Doctor Bartlett?" he asked.

She nodded. Her hostility was gone.

"We don't get much chance to talk in the car pool, Liz, but I've been following *your* work in thermal for a long time. Quite a long time."

She was pleased. "You have?"

"Closely. It's very impressive, Liz."

"You mean that?"

"I do," he said warmly. "It's fresh. It really is. It's innovative."

"I don't know if *you* know, but I've been working on a paper," she told him.

"I didn't. But I'd like to read it. If you'd let me," he added.

"I'd welcome your comments."

"Can we talk about it at lunch?" he asked.

"Just to exchange thoughts . . ." she said.

"Or at dinner," he added.

"I'd like that."

"Tonight?" he asked.

"I'd love it," she replied.

He remembered. "You have that meeting . . ."

"I'll break away early. How about seven?"

"Seven's fine," he replied.

"Better make it seven thirty," she said.

"Seven thirty's perfect," he said.

"Make it quarter to eight," she said.

"Pluperfect," said Wilson.

She gave him the empty coffee cup and turned toward the mouse. "Delicious, Drexel." She left with a promissory smile for Wilson.

"That's some kind of woman," he mused.

The cat said, "She digs you."

"I hope so," said Wilson.

Jake hopped onto the desk, glanced at the

small clock, then whistled. "Looks like you're it, Wilson. I'm running out of time."

Now the voice registered with Wilson. He had heard a voice. Definitely. He glanced around. The radio? Wilson moved to his desk and flicked on the transistor set.

"Spend your sunset years in beautiful Sunrise Homes!" intoned an announcer. "Low mortgages and high living! Golf, swim, dance, jog, sail, tennis, hunt, bowl, fish, scuba, ski, skate, and sculpt!!"

Wilson turned off the set.

"I need your help, Frank," said the cat. His collar was glowing.

Wilson turned and peered at the cat. No, it couldn't be. The cat nodded. Wilson was frozen. A stool crept up from behind and nudged the physicist to sit. He did, with an incredulous look on his face.

Wilson finally managed, "That—was—*you?*"

"It wasn't the mouse," said Jake.

"But your lips aren't moving. I mean, you're not speaking."

"Thought transference, Frank," said the cat. "Nothing exceptional where I came from."

Wilson was still uncomprehending. "I hear it, but I don't believe it."

"My name is Zunar Five Jay slash ninety Doric four seven," said the cat. "But I don't mind your appellation, Jake."

"Zunar? . . ." gasped Wilson. "But you're a *cat!*"

"I should hope so" was the reply. "From a planet you've never heard of, Wilson. I landed yesterday."

Wilson almost stuttered. "I don't believe this."

"I was on a routine mission, Frank—nothing extraordinary. An inspection trip of the colonies. . . ." The cat paused as Wilson shook his head.

"Got hit by a hunk of your space garbage," the cat continued. "You know what you people have floating out there? Positively dangerous!"

Wilson rose. He didn't buy the story.

"*You* were in a *spaceship*, patrolling colonies? . . ."

"It's a dog's life, Frank."

"What kind of colonies?"

"You're on one now," said Jake.

"The earth is one of your . . ."

"For centuries," Jake said. "No need to be frightened. We work through your cats, Frank."

Wilson shook his head. "Slower, Jake. *We* take orders from our *cats?*"

"Don't you?"

The physicist jerked open the door to a small closet. "There's got to be a ventriloquist."

"Really nothing to fear—our foreign policy's benign," said the cat.

"You in there, Link?" Wilson groped through

the clothes hanging in the closet—several lab jackets, a raincoat.

"Plant you now, dig you later."

Wilson whipped around. "Are you saying that cats have ruled this planet for . . ."

"Frank, Frank, Frank," interrupted Jake. "Who did the ancient Egyptians worship—certainly not *dogs*."

Wilson glanced around desperately.

"I know it's you, Link! You're here somewhere!"

"*Cats*," said Jake. "In fact, they built shrines for them. Bastet. Pasht. The Great Cat Ra."

Wilson slammed the closet door shut and yelled toward the ceiling. "Whoever's horsing around . . . it's not funny!"

"*Sit down, Frank*," the cat ordered. His collar emitted an intense light and Wilson found himself back on the stool.

"Your time might not be valuable, but mine is. I'm beginning to lose patience. If you'll listen, I will explain. I do not intend to repeat this, Frank."

Wilson appeared subdued.

"I will be brief." The cat cleared his throat and his manner became professorial. "Frank, man became civilized when he rose off his four legs and developed the dexterity of his fingers. So he wound up with agriculture, the city-state, and backaches. We on our planet, on the other hand, took the shortcut. Not paws, but the *brain*. It's that simple. While you specialized in tools for the land, we specialized in tools for the brain. This collar amplifies brainpower. Without it, Frank, I'm just another cat. Four hundred and thirty I.Q., but just another cat."

Still doubting, Wilson said, "That collar amplifies your . . . ?"

"It provides the energy. Watch."

A deck of playing cards floated up from a workbench and dealt two poker hands. Wilson was flabbergasted. He reached for his cards and studied his hand.

Jake said, "Jacks and nines."

"Beats me," Wilson admitted as he lay down his hand in mid-air. "Pair of eights."

The cards reassembled back into the deck and the pack sailed down to the workbench. Wilson wasn't convinced.

"Okay, so you do card tricks," he said.

"Still skeptical, eh?" said Jake.

The cat glanced around the room. Two model fighter planes of World War II vintage—one American, the other, Luftwaffe—were resting on a shelf. Motors roaring, the duo swooped off and began a miniature hell-for-leather dogfight. Wilson stared in disbelief. The planes zoomed toward him and he just managed to fall to the floor as they swooshed over his right ear. The Luftwaffe, making a sudden loop, was struck by crossfire. It trailed thick black smoke, stalled, faltered and sputtered, then dropped, tail first, into the wastebasket.

Chapter Five

Doctor Frank Wilson lived in a relatively new three-storied apartment complex, tucked away on a cul-de-sac. His own apartment was, as the real estate trade describes, a "bachelor's." There was no bedroom as such, but the place did turn in dog legs and alcoves so that each area was separated from the other.

The tarnished furnishings reflected the occupant. In the living room hung a large tool-shed pegboard which Wilson used as a catchall. On it he hung hats, coats, umbrellas, overshoes, bills, sweaters, letters, tax forms, important reminders, and messages. Any material thing with a hole in it eventually wound up on the board.

A chess table was set up in the living room, but the game had yet to be completed. On the walls were samples of the man's needlepoint. One framed specimen depicted a large-jawed man underwater. He was swallowing a shark.

Next to Wilson's unmade bed was a large ant farm with a NO VACANCY sign tacked to it. The scientist obviously appeared to be working on several highly sophisticated electronic projects. A synthesizer was in the corner. Sheet music and a flute lay atop a dresser. On the shelves in every room were endless stacks of books and pamphlets.

The cat stood on the breakfast counter which divided the kitchen and dining area. He ate voraciously from a dish.

"Delicious," he said when finished, and wiped his mouth with his paw. "What was that stuff, Frank?"

"Chicken liver," said Wilson.

"Tasty," said Jake. "I must remember to take a few cases back with me. Certainly beats the tripe I've been eating." He pushed the dish aside.

"You still haven't answered my question," said Frank.

"Why I selected you?" asked the cat.

He peered at Wilson silently, then said, "Because I like the way you think, Wilson. Your equations rather fascinate me. In fact, they're not bad at all. For a human."

Wilson beamed. "Then I'm on the right track?"

"Not quite," said the cat. "The primal mainstream *is*, as you've surmised, electromagnetic, but not emanating from space, as you've calculated. From the *mind*. Pure *thought*, Frank. It's the source of all energy. Throughout the cosmos, in fact. Manifested, whether it's matter or microwaves, through density. That's common knowledge among the sophisticated nervous systems."

Wilson said, "Then I *am* headed in the right direction?"

"Well, sort of, but years away from a solution," Jake said. "Frank, on my planet we have an expression—'Rub *my* fur and I'll rub *yours.*' How would you like to make a quantum jump?"

"I'd like it."

"You help me," said Jake. "And I'll—as you say—head you in the right direction."

Frank deliberated, but not for long. He extended his hand.

"It's a deal."

The cat said, "Fine. There's no time to lose. Repairs must be made by six twenty-three Sunday for my ship's lift-off. Or *else.*"

"Can you find your way back to the field?"

"Made a memory imprint," nodded Jake.

"With the collar?"

"Right."

"Can any brain use that collar?" asked the physicist.

"Care to try?" The cat smiled.

"You're kidding."

"That's one thing I don't do—kid." He lowered his head and Wilson seized the collar. "Easy, you're choking me! Don't take it off! That's better. Now watch it—without that collar I'm just another cat. You set?"

"Set," said Wilson.

"Think levitation. You're as light as a feather."

Wilson was clenching the collar. "I'm light as a feather," he said.

"You're floating," said Jake.

"I'm floating!" cried Wilson.

Slowly, his feet began to rise off the floor. Now his body was levitated horizontally as he clung to the cat's collar. Jake was jerked up to a chair.

Joyously, Wilson cried, "I'm really floating!" He began to turn and twist.

Suddenly he sank.

"You're not concentrating!" cried the cat.

Wilson wrinkled his brow and concentrated intensely. He was moving back up when Carl Link burst into the apartment. The man, agitated, was clutching a can of beer and a lighted cigar. He strode directly to the TV set and plunked himself in a chair directly in front of it. His concentration shattered, Wilson crashed to the floor.

"Gotta use your set," said Link. He twirled a knob on the TV, did a double take, and turned back to Wilson.

"What were you doing in the air?" he asked.

"Astronaut exercises," explained Wilson.

"Oh," said Link, and returned to the set. He had a habit of not listening to matters that appeared unimportant.

"Look, Link, I'm busy," said Wilson.

"Forget I'm here," said Link.

The picture came on and the audio soared up.

A sports announcer exclaimed, "With only five seconds to go . . ."

Link said, "The last minute of the game and she throws me out of the apartment. One little cigar burn on one lousy chair!" He indicated his cigar. "You can't even spot it—the upholstery's polka dot!" For the first time, he saw the cat. "When'd you get a cat?"

"Jake's a house guest."

"Hi, Jake," said Link.

"Link, I'm going to have to ask you to . . ." From the loudspeaker came the roar of a crowd.

"Celtics' ball!" cried the announcer. "If they make this basket, they win it . . ."

"Win it?" yelped Link. "They were down by six thirty seconds ago!"

"What a comeback!" cried the sports announcer.

"And I gave a point and a half!" said a disgusted Link. "There goes my hundred!"

A Celtic forward dribbled the ball down the court and leaped up to make an easy dunk. But the ball didn't drop in the basket. It flew ten feet back to a Laker guard who tossed it the length of the court. Two points for the Lakers and the buzzer ended the game.

"Unbelievable!" screamed Link. "Did you see *that?*"

Wilson turned off the set and led Link toward the front door. "Okay, out, you've seen your game, Link."

"All the way across the court!"

"Okay, so *out!*"

"I could use another beer."

"Out!" Wilson pushed Link into the hall.

Link cried, "What's going on? Who you hiding in there, Farrah Fawcett-Majors?" The door closed on his face and Wilson pointed toward the set.

"Those last two points! Was that your doing, Jake?" he asked.

The cat nodded. "Any friend of yours is a friend of mine," he said. "Besides, it seemed the fastest way to get rid of the flake. Let's go. I've got less than thirty-six hours to lift-off."

Wilson tucked Jake in his arms and headed for the door. "How are we getting into Hopscotch? It's bound to be guarded."

"Let me worry about it," said the cat. Wilson opened the door.

There stood Doctor Elizabeth Bartlett. She was dressed for dinner. In her arms was a lovely, furry Persian cat. Face to face with this beautiful creature, Jake emitted a low whistle of approval.

"Hi," said Liz.

"Hi," said Wilson, and made a slight gesture of welcome with his fingers.

"This is Lucy Belle," said Liz. "What do you call *him*?"

"Uh—I call him Jake," Wilson replied.

"Jake. Cute. Jake, this is Lucy Belle. Lucy Belle, this is Jake. I thought they might become acquainted while we're out to dinner," she told Wilson.

"Out to *dinner?*" said Wilson vacantly.

"It was tonight, wasn't it?"

"Tonight? You're right. And I was going to call you," lied Wilson. "Something came up. I'm afraid you'll have to give me a raincheck, Liz."

"What happened?" Her smile was wan.

"What happened was—uh . . ."

"It doesn't matter," she said.

"Of course it matters, it matters a lot, Liz—Doctor. Look, you see, what really happened was this . . ."

Jake began to cough and wheeze. Wilson seized the cue.

"Right. See? He took sick," said Wilson. "Look at him. I don't know why. Suddenly—right out of the blue. Sick."

Liz was concerned. "Something *is* wrong with him."

"I think it's the Tasmanian Croup," said Wilson.

Instinctively, Liz pulled Lucy Belle away. The coughing and wheezing continued. Now Lucy Belle was alarmed.

"The poor thing," Liz said. "He sounds *terrible.*"

"Doesn't he, though?"

She stroked Jake, who appeared to like it. He coughed louder.

"Stop milking it," Wilson said softly to the cat. He eased Elizabeth into the hall. "I was just about to rush him to the vet's."

Wilson pressed the button for the elevator.

"There's an excellent vet right here in this building. Doctor Wenger. Lucy Belle adores him," she said. "If you want me to talk to him . . ."

The elevator door opened and Wilson hurried in. "Not necessary, Elizabeth. He prefers a nose and throat man."

"Nose and throat?"

"He's going to be fine, Liz, and I'm sorry about dinner. I'll make it up to you. How about a picnic? Tomorrow?"

"I'd love it," said Liz, and as the elevator door was closing he was repeating: "Tomorrow."

"You handled that situation very well, Frank," Jake said as the elevator descended.

"I don't know. I don't relish lying to Liz. She's an unusual person," said Wilson.

"Her kittycat's not bad either," replied Jake.

Wilson cautioned, "There's plenty of time for that, Jake."

"That's all right for *you* to say, but I've been confined in a spaceship for *five months,* Wilson."

Chapter Six

In the night, no one saw Rupert Stallwood slip into a secluded, darkened phone booth adjacent to a gas station. He made certain no one was watching before he plugged in his earphone to speak into the lighter-transmitter.

"You can thank your lucky stars I'm on your payroll, sir. The general and his staff have been going from one top-level agency to another all afternoon. And now I've tracked them to Hopscotch, sir. *Hopscotch.* That's a mothballed government hangar where—yes, sir. You *do* know what it is? . . . Yes, sir." He laughed lightly. "Naturally, a powerful international organization like yours, Mister Olympus, would know all about . . ."

There was an angry burst from the lighter and Stallwood winced. "Yes, sir! Absolutely, sir!" Another blast. "Get into Hopscotch? But I can't do that, sir—they have guards all around the . . ." And still another blast. "And dogs, sir!!" And another. "Yes, sir, I will, I'll get in, sir! . . ."

He drove a mile, then parked the motorcycle behind a bush and moved stealthily along the electrified barbed wire. In the far distance he could see Hopscotch's centerpiece, the hangar. A tank rattled by on the far side of the fence. Stallwood ducked. It was gone. He crept along the fence in search of a way to break in. No luck. He heard someone approaching. From behind a tree he saw Wilson. What was Wilson doing here? There was a cat in his arms. He crept forward, unobserved. When Wilson moved, he moved. Now Wilson was at an unguarded back gate, heavily padlocked and chained.

"It's locked," Wilson whispered.

"No problem," said Jake.

From somewhere in the black a jeep approached. Wilson slithered back in the tall grass and lay low. Two soldiers were in the jeep. Next to the driver sat a man with an automatic weapon. The jeep stopped. The two men stepped out, tested the locked gate, then returned to their vehicle and moved on. Wilson emerged from the shadows.

"Point me directly at the lock," whispered Jake.

Stallwood observed it all. All but the glowing collar. It was the way Wilson was holding the cat, tucked deep in his arms. He pointed the cat directly at the heavy chains and the padlocks. They burst open.

Stallwood gasped. He couldn't believe it. But Wilson and the cat were now in the base and swiftly running forward, avoiding vehicles that cruised the grounds. When they reached the hangar, Stallwood was no more than fifty feet behind them. He hid behind some steel drumheads. What was Wilson up to? And why the cat? He watched as Wilson, the cat still tucked securely in his arms, climbed a ladder. From a window high above the ground, they were peering into the hangar.

Seemingly, the spaceship was still intact. General Stilton and his aides were bending over a long folding table covered with scraps of paper—notes and roughly drawn diagrams. Empty paper coffee cups and the wrappings of inedible sandwiches were strewn about. Bright-eyed and bushytailed, Stilton whacked his crop against his thigh as he addressed an exhausted NASA executive and his assistants.

"Well?" he cried.

"Not much so far," said the weary NASA chief. "A few bits of fine hair . . . a broken fingernail. . . . We've taken the measurements of the molded seats for body shape . . . computed the height and distance from the seat of the instrument panel to determine the arm length of the . . . the . . . pilot. That together with a number of other factors will be fed into the computer at headquarters. In a day or two, we might have an idea what he looks like."

Stilton whacked his crop across the table.

"No time!" he cried. "I want a mobile computer brought here first thing in the morning! Colonel!"

"Captain!" cried the colonel.

"*Ser---geant!*" bellowed the captain.

Sergeant Duffy began scribbling on his note-pad.

"With double-pronto input!" cried the general.

"Double pronto, sir!" boomed the colonel.

"*Double pronto!*" echoed the captain.

"Fast," wrote the sergeant.

The general snapped his crop and abruptly strode out of the hangar, tailed with military precision by his aides. At the front gate soldiers snapped to attention and saluted. The command car shot out of the base. It was followed by the NASA staff car.

"All clear," Wilson said to Jake softly.

He climbed down the ladder and, holding the cat securely, crept up to the entrance of the hangar. A guard and his dog patrolled back and forth. The dog stopped, snarled, then, barking, rushed toward Wilson. Jake's collar glowed. Instantaneously, the dog and his master became immobile.

"Wears off in twenty minutes," Jake whispered to Wilson. "Harmless. Won't remember a thing. Let's get moving."

He leaped out of the physicist's arms and bounded into the hangar with Wilson directly behind. Stallwood watched with disbelieving eyes.

Something wild was going on. He *had* to see what they were up to. But he didn't dare risk going through the front entrance. He climbed up the ladder and tried the window Wilson had used.

The view was limited, but at least he could see something. There were Wilson and the cat climbing into the spaceship's cabin. Once in, they were obscured.

Stallwood became desperate. He glanced about for a better vantage point. The metal ladder welded to the side of the hangar offered prospects. It continued up the roof of the hangar. Stallwood hesitated, then began to climb. High above the ground, from a prone position on top of the curved roof, he found a crack. He peeked. A much better view. He could see Wilson from here, but not the cat. But at least that was something.

Wilson, halfway out of the cabin, was an interested bystander to something Jake was doing in the craft.

There was the "artichoke," a foot above its pinnacle. It gleamed with a low aura, but it was not turning. Jake busied himself with a computerlike device built into the control panel. The printout was in a language that resembled hieroglyphics. Strange, unearthly tools could be seen in an exposed compartment as Jake's collar glowed.

"Okay," said Jake. "First we have to disengage the transducer switch. Use that wrench and get on top of the ship. Coordinate with *me*."

"How do I get up there?" Wilson asked.

The cat touched a spot on the inner wall of the console. A flap opened. There, in a pocket, was a spare cat collar, identical to that Jake was wearing. It was held in place by what appeared to be a miniature tire rim.

"Use the spare," said Jake. "You know what to do. Concentrate."

Wilson grasped the spare collar. He closed his eyes and concentrated. There were furrows in his brow. He gritted his teeth and felt a twinge in his body. Something was happening—he could feel it. His feet began to move, then rise. They rose above his head and pulled the rest of his body. A look of incredulous joy was on the man's face as, feet first, he moved, in fits and spurts, toward the top of the ship.

Stallwood looked on with utter amazement. Wilson was flying with a glowing cat collar in his hand.

At the front gate the garbage-collection truck arrived for its nightly pickup. The driver, a stolid, phlegmatic sort, braked to a stop for recognition.

"What's going on here, Hal?" he asked the guard. "The joint's buzzin'. What's the excitement?"

"I can't talk, Red," replied the guard. "But just don't take any pictures."

"Of what . . . trash cans?" replied the garbage collector.

"All I know is I got orders. I have to accompany you, Red. Follow me." The soldier leaped into his jeep and it moved into the base followed directly by the garbage truck.

Wilson, upside down, wielded an odd-shaped wrench around a long sprocket on top of the ship.

"Okay!" yelled Jake. "Now when the switch beeps, turn it! You ready?"

"Ready!" cried Wilson.

The switch beeped. Wilson jerked the wrench and the switch lit up.

"Got a positive!" yelled Jake. "Nice going! Come on down!"

But Wilson's strong tug had sent him sailing far out and around the ship.

"Jake!" he screamed. Now he was down, up, swooping sideways. He was completely out of control. Terrified, he managed to plop into the cabin with a soft landing. Jake displayed no concern. In fact, he was reading the printout on a "window" on the computer.

"Thought so," said Jake. "The focal terminal in the microtransformer's vaporized. Happens in these older models."

"You sure?" Wilson said, still panting.

"Positive. But I'll double-check."

A metal door, one inch square, slid aside at

the base of the bulkhead. There was the micro-transformer, intricately connected to wires. Jake opened a flap on the transformer, exposing an area the size of a thimble.

"Just what I thought," said Jake.

"That's where the focal terminal goes?" asked Wilson. "In that little thing?"

"Acts as a catalyzer," Jake replied. "I'll need about six cubits of Org twelve."

"What's Org twelve?"

"What the focal terminal's made of," was the reply. "Just need a strand. For emergency repair. You don't have Org twelve on this planet?"

"Is it like mayonnaise?"

"You probably call it by a different name. Stand back," the cat ordered. Wilson drew aside and Jake began to work on the computer. It was noticeable now—the intensity of the light in his collar was stronger.

The jeep stopped suddenly and the garbage truck squealed to a stop. In the darkness it was hard to tell, but something appeared out of place to the soldier. Almost directly ahead of his jeep, near the entrance to the hangar, were a soldier and his dog. They seemed immobile. Not a sound or movement from them. The driver edged cautiously from the jeep, then stopped.

"You all right, Tom?" he asked. There was no response.

He moved several steps forward. "Hey, Tom!"

he cried. Not a word from his friend. Or the dog. Nothing.

Jake read the printout aloud as Wilson tucked the spare collar back into its pocket and closed the flap.

"Org twelve," Jake read. "Ductile, yellow metallic element. Melting point: one thousand sixty-three. Tensile strength: nineteen thousand . . ."

Wilson had his suspicions. "Tensile strength what?"

"Nineteen thousand."

The computer printed another message. Jake read it.

"Atomic weight: one nine six point nine six seven," he said, and Wilson's eyes popped open.

"Wait a minute!" he cried. "That's the atomic weight of gold!"

The soldier, an arm's length away, cautiously touched his buddy. Now he ran his fingers over the dog.

"Holy cow!" he whispered. He fled to the closest alarm box.

The driver of the garbage truck poked his head out of his cabin. "What's goin' on, Hal?"

Jake peered intently at the computer printout. Now it steadied and a reading flashed in one corner of the eye-screen.

"Right," he said. "Checks out—it's gold."

"Oh, boy," said Wilson.

"Will it be difficult to lay our hands on?"

"You kidding?!"

An alarm bell wailed. It was joined by another, and another. Searchlights stabbed the darkness, probing.

"They're on to us!" Wilson cried.

"Follow me!" said Jake. He leaped from the ship as Wilson climbed down.

"Over here!" cried Jake. Wilson was six feet behind as they reached the hangar's opening. A beam of light found them. They stood frozen. Jake's collar glowed. The cat peered directly at the searchlight's source. The searchlight exploded.

"You can't zap the whole garrison!" cried Wilson. "Let's get out of here!"

The cat knew his limitations. "This way!" he cried. He swirled out of the hangar with Wilson on his tail. More soldiers. A siren began to moan, joined by others. Surrounding them, the sound of weapons carriers. Men shouting. Jeeps. Dogs. Tanks. Searchlights circled the base. The mounting thunder of crisscrossing half-tracks and motorcycles mingled with the squeals of tires and the clank of armor. Clouds of dust.

"They're over here!" someone cried.

The garbage truck, caught in the middle of the pandemonium, tried elusive measures, turning right, then left, then a U. A jeep bore down on Wilson and Jake. The cat focused on it. The car wheeled into an abrupt one-hundred-eighty-degree turn, as if on a spinning turntable, and whipped out of sight.

"Into the barrel, Frank!" cried Jake.

Wilson jumped into an empty metal drum. It lay near the hangar.

A searchlight pinpointed the cat. The cat pinpointed the searchlight. An explosion and splinters. One by one, the searchlights blew skyward. Jake was aiming at a tank when he was grasped from behind. The cat slithered free, but his collar was gone, and in the soldier's hands it had lost its luster. Not ten feet away, a half-track swept down on Jake. He leaped aboard.

A screeching motorcycle cut sharply to avoid hitting a jeep. It tipped over Wilson's barrel and set it in motion. It rolled rapidly toward two oncoming tanks. Jake's collar was gone, but not his ingenuity. He hopped toward the light and gave himself up. The tanks swerved to destroy him, missed, and narrowly skinned the metal drum. The garbage truck screamed into a spin, bounced into a tank, and spun away, crashing into the hangar.

From the roof could be heard a long, piercing scream. Stallwood, shaken loose by the collision, came sliding down the roof. He dropped into the open-faced, half-filled garbage loader, and lay groaning.

Wilson crawled out of the barrel. In front of him sat a riderless motorcycle. He ran for it.

One hundred feet away an officer was questioning a soldier.

"You sure it was a cat?" he asked.

The soldier held up the cat's collar. "Here's his collar, sir!"

From nowhere, Jake leaped, poked his head into the collar, and darted off.

"Jake!" cried Wilson. He couldn't see the cat. In the distance he caught a glimpse of a glowing collar. The motorcycle roared toward it.

"Jake!" cried Wilson. The cat leaped onto the physicist's back as the cycle shot toward the barrier near the guard house.

"Do your stuff, Jake!" yelled Wilson.

The collar was in white heat as the cycle rose and zoomed over the barrier. A popeyed guard flattened to the ground.

From a secluded phone booth in the corridor of the emergency ward of a hospital, Stallwood, his head heavily bandaged, spoke with hushed excitement into his lighter-transmitter.

"I know it sounds unbelievable, Mister Olympus, but it's absolutely true—I saw it with my own eyes. . . . *My* eyes? . . . Excellent, sir, twenty-twenty vision, have them checked annually. . . . Yes, sir, yes, sir, . . . but I *am* telling you the truth. . . . Scout's honor, . . . a Tenderfoot, sir, but I was making rapid strides toward an Eagle when . . . sir? . . . sir? . . . I repeat, sir, a magic collar that defies gravity. It lights up and flies him all over the place. . . . Would I lie to you, sir? . . . And all this time *we* thought he was down in his basement playing with his mouse. Oh, that Wilson's diabolically clever, sir. Do you know where he hides the collar? Around his *cat's* neck. . . . Believe me, sir . . . with these own eyes . . . I swear on the grave of my dear, departed father, sir. . . . Well, not yet, sir, but he *is* failing, in *very* poor health, sir. . . . Proof? . . . How can I get proof, sir? I mean, what you are asking. . . . Yes, sir, I will, sir, proof is what you shall get, sir!"

Chapter Seven

Wilson and the cat were up early the next morning. The weary physicist sat at a table with a slide rule and pocket calculator, wrestling with a problem. Jake, on the breakfast counter, was engrossed with his breakfast. He licked the dish clean, then dropped to his haunches.

"This is even better than the stuff I had last night," Jake said. "What's it called?"

"Tuna," said Wilson, intent with his slide rule. He tossed a pencil on the table. "It keeps coming out the same way. It doesn't make sense."

"What's the problem?"

"According to your figures, we're going to need a hundred and twenty thousand dollars' worth of gold."

"So?"

"So! Jake, forgetting the money, which I can't, you know how much gold that is? That much." Wilson spread his arms apart, indicating a good-sized pile. "And you want to put it in a thing that

86

big?" He indicated the space in the thimble-sized transducer.

"Relax. You people still operate on the bulk system as opposed to psi content. I'll reduce it to the size I need and still retain its properties."

"How?"

"How? With the collar and Zelatoid compression."

"What's Zelatoid . . . ?"

The cat interrupted. "Frank, I don't have time to go into these things. I have exactly nineteen hours, thirty-six minutes to lift-off, and you keep asking questions. Let's get the gold."

Wilson was impatient. "Will you please tell me *how?* To buy a hundred and twenty thousand dollars' worth of gold on *this* planet, you need one hundred and twenty thousand dollars."

"Is that a problem?"

"A problem? My total capital is tied up in my next salary check. And if you're interested, that amounts to exactly . . ."

"Spare me," said the cat. "It's not of importance. We will get the money. Believe me, Wilson. Because if you think that I'm going to spend the rest of my nine lives on this miserable globe, you've got another think coming."

Stallwood, a small movie camera hanging around his neck, peered furtively down the apartment courtyard. It was his first visit to Wilson's complex. He had found the physicist's name in the hall, above the mailbox, then checked to spot the exact location of Wilson's apartment. He had to be sure. Proof was what Mister Olympus wanted, and proof was what he would get.

He walked quietly down the pathway, passed the fountain, and moved on. There it was—Wilson's apartment—on the third floor. Not much could be seen from the courtyard. A trellis stretched across the brick of the building opposite Wilson's. Stallwood glanced up and down. No one was coming. He moved quickly and began to climb the trellis. Halfway up, he became conscious of someone watching. Two tight-lipped, middle-aged women, carrying shopping bags, stared at him with disapproval.

"Birdwatching," Stallwood said lamely.

The women muttered. He began his descent.

He touched the lawn and tipped his hat. "Ladies." Their stare was icy. "Yes . . . well . . . lovely morning. . . . I see you've been shopping . . . isn't the cost of living beastly? . . ."

He pointed, as if spotting a bird. "Oh, ho!" he cried. "There you are! You little rascal, you!" And he dashed after the imaginary bird.

The women were not fooled. When he had disappeared around the corner of the building, they began clucking.

Wilson paced up and down his living room.

"No, no, no!" he said. "That's final, Jake! No. *N-O!*"

"But . . ." began Jake.

"Have you ever heard of patriotism, Jake? *I'm a loyal American, Jake. Loyal. I will not break into Fort Knox.*"

"Then the alternative is . . ."

"*And I will not break into banks!* If you need gold so badly, Jake, make it yourself!"

"I'm not a magician," said Jake.

Carl Link burst into the apartment carrying a small gym bag. He plunked himself in the chair in front of the TV set and turned the knob.

Wilson stared at him. "What're you doing?"

Link drew the chair closer to the set. "Borrowing your TV. Just bring me a beer and forget I'm around."

"Forget you're around! You're *here!*"

From his gym bag Link withdrew his TV-watching equipment—a handful of cigars, a bunch of matches, and a sack of peanuts, plus an ashtray. He placed them for his convenience on a nearby coffee table, then lit up a stogie.

"May I inquire . . . ?" began Wilson.

The racetrack announcer said, "The horses are on the track . . ."

"I've had enough inquiries for one day, Wilson. You mind? Make yourself at home," Link told Frank.

"Link . . ." began Wilson.

"Please," Link interrupted. "My wife's made up an equitable TV schedule for the day—now let's abide by it. The Peachtree Derby and the football games on your set, the Metropolitan Opera on mine."

"Can't you see I'm busy?" said Wilson.

"Doing what? Playing with your pussycat?"

"Link . . ."

The garbage expert motioned for Wilson to quiet down. "Please. I've got a bundle on the Peachtree, Franklin."

In the courtyard below, Stallwood poked his head around the corner of a building. The women were gone. He glanced up at the walkway that spanned the two buildings. That's where he could get his pictures. Up on that ledge, above Wilson's apartment. He sprang onto the stairway and took the stairs two at a time. Now he was on the walkway. He looked back, and around. All clear.

Wilson was still having no luck with his friend. "I'm sorry, Link, but . . ."

"Ssssh," said Link.

From the set came the announcer: ". . . exclusively for two-year-olds. Plus some three- and some four-year-olds. . . ." The picture was bright and clear. The horses were moving into the starting gate.

Link pulled up a hassock and plunked his feet up.

"Okay, Lucky Jake, let's go!"

"Lucky Jake?" inquired Wilson.

"It's a hunch bet. A hundred on the nose at fifteen to one."

Jake perked up. He leaped onto the chair alongside Link and peered at the TV screen.

"If he comes in, Tiger," said Link, stroking the cat, "I'll be fifteen hundred in front and you'll be licking mackerel filets." He glanced around. "Did you forget my beer or did I drink it?" He rose. "Never mind, I'll get it." He strode into the kitchen.

Wilson whispered, "I'll try to get rid of him."

"Wait, wait, wait," said the cat. "You hear what he said, Frank? If Lucky Jake finishes first, he wins fifteen hundred dollars."

"So?"

"So if Link can win fifteen hundred, why can't he win a hundred and twenty thousand?"

"You don't understand," said Wilson. "He *made* a bet, he hasn't *won* it."

"He will," said Jake.

Link walked in, popping a fresh can of beer. "You can afford better stuff than this, Wilson."

He fell into the chair and admonished, "Now a little peace and quiet, please. I got everything riding on this nag."

"The horses are at the post . . ." said the announcer.

No one saw Stallwood. His head, upside down, peered into the living room through the top of Wilson's window. He had scrambled onto a ledge directly above Wilson's apartment. The head withdrew. Stallwood began to get his camera ready. He struggled with the film. Mechanics were not his forte.

"And they're off!" cried the announcer. "It's Sue Me on top with Madeline and Sweet Prince on the rail! Attaboy on the outside . . ."

The horses were in a close, fast, dusty race. All but one.

"Lucky Jake is still in the gate!" cried the announcer. "No, here he comes, folks . . . oops, he's stopped! . . ."

Lucky Jake strolled over to the rail and began nibbling on grass.

"He's stopped for lunch," said the announcer.

Link said, "I don't believe this." He stood up. "Eat on your own time, Muttonhead!"

Frantically, Lucky Jake's jockey jerked the horse aside and headed him down the track. The animal loped.

Now the horses approached the far turn, bunched up on the stretch. Thirty yards ahead of them was Lucky Jake. He was going to be lapped.

"Bunched up around the far turn and into the stretch they come!" cried the announcer. "Lucky Jake's moving, folks, but at this rate, he'll finish Thursday!"

Jake's collar began to glow.

"I should have bet on the Metropolitan Opera!" muttered Link. He rose, then looked at Jake with disdain. *"Lucky Jake!"*

"They're moving into the turn and . . ." The announcer hesitated. "Wait—one minute. Hold everything, I—don't—believe—it. *I—don't—believe—it!*"

Link turned back to the set. No wonder the announcer was so excited. Lucky Jake was whirling around the track with the speed of a bullet. Now he was only a few yards behind the other horses. They were nearing the finish line.

"Unbelievable!" cried the incredulous announcer.

Lucky Jake flew by the other horses.

"It's Lucky Jake! By five lengths!" The announcer was hysterical. Link did an ecstatic jig around the room.

Stallwood was standing on the ledge and tried focusing his camera on Wilson's apartment. But he couldn't see a thing from that position. He tried squatting on his knees. That wasn't ideal, but it was better.

"Fifteen hundred smackeroos!" yelped Link. He kissed the TV set. "From now on, baby, I watch every game on you! That calls for another beer! How about you, Wilson, I'm buying."

"No thanks."

"Incidentally," Link said. "You could use another six-pack." Skipping nimbly, Link danced into the kitchen.

"You did all that? On TV?" Wilson asked the cat.

"If I can see it, I can control it, Frank." He began to pace, then stopped. "I have an idea."

"Let me guess," said Wilson.

"I think our gold problem's solved."

"Count me out, Jake," said Wilson. "Besides, it won't work."

"Frank, you're looking at a desperate cat!"

"But I don't know anything about placing a bet. I wouldn't even know *where* to do it."

Link airily moved from the kitchen with an opened beer can. "What a start. I've a feeling I'm going to murder 'em on the football games."

Jake said, "I guess we're going to have to take in another partner."

"Who?" asked Wilson.

"Him."

Link said, "Did you say something, Frank?"

Wilson ignored him. "Link? Do you think that's wise?"

"Do you think what's wise?" asked Link. "Who're you talking to?"

"But . . ." began Wilson.

"Who're you talking to?" asked the bewildered Link.

"Ask him," Jake said to Wilson.

"Frank?" Link was puzzled. He moved toward Wilson for a closer look.

"It's crazy," said Wilson.

"Old buddy?" said Link, peering into the physicist's face.

"What?"

"Who?" said Link.

"Link, how many football games on TV today?"

"Three pro games. East, Midwest, Far West. Who?"

"Brief him," said Jake.

"You feeling okay?" Link was worried.

"I don't think it's a good idea, but okay," said Wilson.

"You know, if I didn't know better, I'd say you were talking to the cat," Link said.

"I was," said Wilson. Link stared at him.

"Right," Link finally said. "Listen, my friend, it can happen to anyone in government service. That's why they have staff psychiatrists. First thing Monday . . ."

Wilson interrupted. "Link, take a deep breath." He paused. "Remember that artichoke?"

Stallwood was on his knees, on the ledge, with the movie camera upside down. It was the only way he could get his shots, by bending far over. Wilson's windows were closed. Stallwood couldn't hear a word they were saying, but he could follow the movements of Wilson, Link, and the cat. He began taking pictures.

It seemed that Wilson was explaining something to Link, who looked at his friend as if he were crazy. Whatever Wilson was saying, Link wasn't buying. He poured beer into a mug. Now the cat's collar began to glow. The beer jumped back from the mug into the can. Link hesitated, then shook his head in disbelief. He poured again. Same result. He peered into the can with bewilderment and was squirted with an eyeful of beer. Drenched, he ran to the kitchen and reached for a paper towel.

On his knees, Stallwood scurried along the ledge. He would have to shoot this from another window. Upside down. There, fine. An excellent shot. Link was drying himself with a paper towel. Or trying to. He was having problems. As he pulled the towel off the roller, it retracted like a rubber band. He made several efforts. The cat's collar was still glowing. Link, in desperation, yanked the towel. It wound around him, from feet to head. He was bound like an Egyptian mummy. Struggling, Link edged out of the kitchen in terror, the cat and Wilson directly behind.

Stallwood scurried to another section of the ledge. Ah, there they were. He began to shoot just as Link was wafted into the air and slowly deposited in a chair. The camera ran out of film.

On his knees, Stallwood scurried back to his supplies. He began to reload when he glanced up. He was directly in front of the two ladies' apartment. One held a revolver. It pointed directly at his head. The woman was trembling. Her hand was unsteady. Behind her was her sister.

"Sick, sick, sick," the woman kept repeating.

The one holding the revolver cried, "Hands up, Buster!"

"Let me explain, ladies!" Stallwood said.

"Sick!" cried the sister and the other placed the gun directly between Stallwood's eyes.

"We're not fooling!" she cried.

Stallwood raised his arms.

"Call the police, Edna!" ordered the woman with the revolver.

Chapter Eight

The smoke-filled, run-down pool hall contained not only the usual pocket pool tables but several billiard tables. A match was being played and a small group of sullen pool hall habitués were gathered to kibitz.

But they were silent now. That was the way Earnest Ernie wanted it. And what Earnest Ernie wanted, Earnest Ernie usually got. After all, he owned the joint. But it was more than just that. He had gotten to the top the hard way and had stayed here because of sagacity, size, and sass. Few shook his tree now, or even dared.

A middle-aged, bookie-entrepreneur, Earnest Ernie wore his bashed-in nose as a badge of distinction. To go with it, he had cauliflower ears, squinting eyes, and a nervous mouth, the combination of which all spelled "crook." Lucky for everyone, really, that Honest Harry was around.

Now *there* was a man you could trust. An aging, weathered repository of skullduggery, Honest Harry spent most of his daylight hours in

Ernie's pool hall. And a good portion of the night, too, getting an edge here, taking an edge there. A guy had to live. But you could always depend on Honest Harry because he had credibility. The guy was fair.

The match in progress was a typical Earnest Ernie setup. Only a fool, or a sucker, would want to lock horns with Sarasota Slim. The man was a master. An uncommunicative sort, Earnest Ernie's hand-picked pool hustler wore a wide-brimmed hat pushed back over his head and constantly combed a cowlick. Seldom did his eyes reveal emotion.

Weasel, Ernie's sidekick partner, couldn't suppress his glee as he watched Sarasota Slim wrap up the game with some beautifully executed shots.

The phone rang in the nearby decrepit office. Runtlike Weasel shuffled off to answer it.

"You're down two hundred, Sucker," said Ernie. "Y'want to double it?"

"Earnest Ernie's Sportin' Club, Weasel speakin'. What's your pleasure?" the man asked on the phone.

The Sucker glanced at Ernie. "You give me four balls, I double it."

"Wha'd'ye say, Sarasota?" asked Ernie.

"I say give him *five*," replied Slim.

"Make it fast, Link," Weasel said into the phone. "We got a hot one on the rotisserie."

The Sucker placed his money on the table and Ernie passed it to Honest Harry.

"Honest Harry holds," he said. The Sucker glanced at Honest Harry. He had his doubts.

"Can I trust him?" the Sucker said.

"Would a crook have a name like Honest Harry?" said Ernie. "Break, Sucker."

"You wanna bet *what?*" Weasel was saying on the phone.

The Sucker broke the balls and none rolled in any pockets. Sarasota Slim coolly chalked up and prepared to do his thing.

Weasel held one hand over the phone's mouthpiece. "Hey, Ernie," he said. "Link wants to take his winnin's on Lucky Jake and parlay the three football games."

"Guy's livin' high. Three game parlay."

"It's one hundred and twenty G's if he makes it."

Ernie waved his approval. "Takin' candy from a baby, Weasel."

Weasel returned to the phone. "Deal, Link." He hung up and made a note of the transaction as he ambled back toward Ernie. Sarasota Slim was methodically cleaning up the table.

"One born every minute," said Weasel.

Sarasota Slim leaned over the pool table. He said, "Five ball in the pocket . . . fourteen in the side . . . and nine in the corner." He proceeded to make all three.

Ernie beamed as Honest Harry handed him the winnings. "We gotta think of ourselves as therapists," said Ernie.

Chapter Nine

General Stilton was not a man to be concerned with yesterdays. Last night's bungling at Hopscotch was done, finis, and there was nothing he could do about it now. But something could be done about *today,* and he was doing it.

He had brought the "brains" of the country to the hangar and they were working against time. Under the direction of the general and aides, they bustled about, busy with their assignments. Several technicians worked in trailers housing mobile computers while others studied the spaceship for telltale clues and fingerprinting.

Colonel Woodruff stepped swiftly to the general, brushing Doctor Heffel aside.

"Fingerprints, General! They found fingerprints!" He handed his superior several sheets.

"Well, now!" beamed the general as he studied them.

"On top of the hull, sir!" said the colonel. "In the cabin! Everywhere! They're the fingerprints of a man, General!"

The general cracked his riding crop against his thigh.

"In other words, whoever brought this ship here was aided and abetted by some disloyal American! Gentlemen, we're dealing with a collaborator!" Stilton thrust the print into Sergeant Duffy's hands.

"I want the name that goes with these prints! Put it through the computer!"

"Double pronto, sir!"

Duffy handed the papers to a nearby computer operator and gave him instructions. The information was programmed into the clacking computer as Captain Anderson made his appearance. He was holding a small envelope.

"They've found more, sir! Look!" He handed the envelope to the general, who opened the flap and peered in.

"What the blazes is this?"

"Fine hair, sir!" replied the captain. "The pilot wears a fur coat!"

General Stilton stared at him with disdain. Anderson was oblivious to this. He held a sheet with prints directly in front of the general's eyes.

"Even *more* important, sir, tiny prints! Around a claw formation! You know, kind of like a pussycat's!"

This was the last straw for the general.

"Pussycat's!!" he fumed. Stilton turned and yelled at the technicians. "Why aren't I hearing some tickety-tacs?"

The computers swept into a crescendo of noise and flicking colored lights. A readout appeared on one of the monitors. Stilton bent to read.

". . . fingerprints of Doctor Frank Wilson!" he muttered, "Social Security Number: 631–07–0829! Doctorate, Cal Tech!"

"That's *my* Doctor Wilson!" cried Heffel.

"The scoundrel!" thundered the general.

Someone from military intelligence said, "We'll have him in the slammer in an hour, General!"

"And blow the whole ball game!" cried the general. A plan was forming in his mind. He was pleased with himself as he smacked his riding crop.

"Gentlemen," he said. "We're after Mister Big. And this double-crossing fink is going to lead us to him. To find the rat, tail the cat."

Heffel was mystified. "The cat?"

"Just an expression, Heffel," said the general.

Back in Wilson's apartment, the atmosphere was one of optimism. Not quite bordering on jubilance, but that time would come, they were certain. The Rams had just beaten the New England Patriots, and there were only two more games to go. If ever there was a cinch, this was it. With Jake around, they couldn't miss.

"Final score, Rams twenty-six, Patriots seventeen," said the announcer on TV.

Jake was reclining on the back of Link's chair.

He alternated between watching the game and grooming himself. A routine day.

"One down, two to go!" said Wilson happily.

"And without your help, Jake," said Link. "This calls for another six-pack." He moved toward the kitchen. "What'll you have, Jake?"

Jake said, "Make mine chopped herring."

Wilson twirled the dial for the Houston Oilers–Chicago game.

The announcer was saying, ". . . last quarter, with the Oilers leading the Bears twenty-one to twelve . . ."

"We're still leading, twenty-one to twelve," said Link.

A knock on the door.

"Come in!" Wilson cried.

Liz did. She was carrying a picnic basket and was obviously dressed for picnicking, for she wore tight jeans and a pullover. In the other hand, she grasped a cat carrier, where lay sexy, inviting Lucy Belle. The Persian arched back, scanned the room with sultry eyes, and caught a glimpse of Jake. She purred.

"Lucy Belle insisted on coming," said Liz.

"Coming?" asked Wilson. His mind wasn't in focus.

"To the picnic."

"Oh." Now Wilson remembered. "The picnic . . ." Very nice, but some other time. It showed on his face.

107

Liz was puzzled. "What's wrong? Is his croup worse?"

"Whose croup's worse?"

"Jake's."

"Yes, it is. I was up all night with him," said Wilson, seizing the cue.

"Goodness."

Wilson overplayed his hand. "I think it's gone into hyperzemia."

"What's hyperzemia?" she asked.

"What Jake's got."

Jake crossed his eyes and began to wheeze.

"What'd your doctor do for him yesterday?" Liz asked.

"Gave him two aspirin."

She was horrified. "Two aspirin!"

A roar from the TV and Link rushed in from the kitchen.

"What's that? What happened?"

Another thundering roar from the crowd. Wilson turned toward the set.

". . . with the score now twenty-one to nineteen in favor of Houston!" cried the announcer.

"Twenty-one to nineteen—how'd they score?" cried Link.

"How should I know?" yelled Wilson. Both looped back to the set.

"Two aspirin is ridiculous!" Liz exclaimed. No reaction. Their backs were toward her. "No wonder he's feeling worse!" They weren't listening. "I'll be right back! He needs an expert!"

She placed the cat carrier on the floor and left. Jake jumped down and ambled over to the Persian. Through the wire mesh, they rubbed noses.

"The Bears have the ball!" Wilson cried.

"Interception, Jake!" Link screamed. "The Bears have the ball!"

"Stop that guy!" Wilson screamed at the screen. "He's going all the way!"

"Stop him!" Wilson cried. "Jake!"

"He's out of bounds! Out of bounds on the thirty!" cried Link.

Wilson turned. No Jake. Where was he? Clear across the room, meowing at that stupid Lucy Belle.

"Problems, Jake!" cried Wilson.

Jake peered at him and said, "Relax. Plenty of time, Frank," then returned to his love. "Hi, Sweetie. Can I get you anything?"

Link got in the act. "They're within field goal range, Jake!"

"If they make this, we're sunk!" cried Wilson.

"Stop working yourself into a lather," Jake cautioned. "Believe me. Relax." He returned to Lucy Belle. "A little tuna, honey?"

"Tuna? You out of your mind, Jake?"

A whistle blew.

"Time out!" said Link.

The door opened and in walked Liz with Doctor Wenger. He was not too pleased to be there— that much was obvious. A middle-aged man wearing a loud Hawaiian shirt, blatant shorts, and sandals, the veterinarian was protesting.

"At least you could have waited till this game was over," the vet said. "I've got ten bucks on Chicago." Wenger's face brightened. "Oh. You've got a set. You have it on. What's happening?"

"Time out," Wilson said. "May I speak to you alone, Jake?" The cat ignored him.

"I'm glad I didn't miss anything," said the vet.

Liz said, "This is Doctor Wenger, fellows." No reply. Their backs were toward him. Liz picked up Jake and placed him on a table.

"What're you doing?" asked Wilson.

"Here's your patient, Doctor. I definitely believe he needs attention," she said.

"Attention, eh?" Wenger said with one eye glancing at the set. He began a routine examination of the cat without looking at him.

"How'd they get to the thirty?" asked Wenger.

"Interception," said Link.

"While we were in the elevator?" said the vet. "You see—we missed an *interception*," he accused Elizabeth.

The referee set the ball in place and called for action. Jake squirmed to keep his eye on the set. His view was obstructed. It became increasingly difficult for Wenger to hold the cat.

"Whoa, boy," said the doctor.

The announcer said, "Time's back in. What's Chicago going to do? Go for a pass—or try for a field goal?"

"What do you think, Doctor?" Liz asked anxiously.

"They should try for a field goal," replied Wenger.

"About the *cat!*" she said impatiently.

"Oh. Tense. Very tense," said Wenger. "Neck muscles all bunched up."

An ascending roar from the crowd.

"They're moving out of the huddle . . ." said the announcer.

"He's going to choke in that collar," said Liz, and before Jake could react, she had slipped it off his neck. Jake's eyes widened. His frantic meows were swallowed by the roar of the crowd.

"They're going for a field goal!" cried the announcer.

"Go, Chicago!" said Wenger.

"And with only twenty seconds to play! If they make this, it's all but over, folks," cried the announcer. "All over!"

"Stop 'em!" cried Wilson, while Link yelled, "Block it! Block that kick!"

Jake squirmed frantically. It was almost impossible for the veterinarian to hold him.

"This cat's unbelievable. *Hold him!*" Wenger instructed Liz.

"I'm trying!"

"Strong as an ox!"

Liz took a firm stance and a tight two-armed hold as the doctor quickly reached for his bag. His eyes were still on the game. He brought out a hypodermic needle and a vial.

"Do your stuff, Jake!" cried Wilson. His eyes were riveted to the set. He turned. Wenger was preparing the shot.

"Hey! What're you doing? Where's his collar?" cried Wilson.

Now Link glanced back. "Where's whose . . ."

They both leaped to their feet and Wilson scrambled over the couch.

"What's going on here?"

"He's hypermanic!" cried the doctor.

"You can't do that, man!" cried Link.

"Giving him a sedative," said Wenger. "Please, you're blocking the set!"

"Where's his collar?" cried Wilson.

Liz reassured him. "The doctor knows what he's doing, Frank . . ."

"The center is down on the ball," said the announcer.

Wilson tore the collar out of Liz's hand. "Sorry, Liz . . ." His efforts to slip the collar around Jake's neck failed. The vet's needle was poised.

"Let go of that cat," Wenger instructed.

"*You* let go!" said Wilson.

The men struggled. The needle was inches away from the cat's backside.

". . . and the ball's snapped!" cried the announcer. All eyes were on the set.

"Jake!" screamed Link.

"Stop it, Frank! Frank!" Liz cried.

"The kick's in the air!" cried the announcer just as Wilson shoved Liz aside and slipped the collar over Jake's neck. Jake whirled and faced the picture. The collar glowed to white heat and Doctor Wenger, his arm freed, plunged the needle into Jake's rear.

The football, on its way over the crossbar, dropped like a stone, bounced twice on the crossbar, and rolled back to the one-yard line.

Now the collar began to glow, then spark. The TV picture erupted into crazy, wild patterns. The picture was not only lost but began to beam. A PLEASE STAND BY logo appeared on the screen.

The announcer was hysterical. "No good! The kick's no good! *The—kick's—no—good!*"

Jake's eyes began to glaze. He felt lightheaded.

Link was dancing with joy. "We won it, we won it!"

"Oh, boy . . ." Jake said weakly. He felt sick. His eyes blurred and he fainted.

Wilson looked at him. "What is it? Jake?" There was no response. He cradled the cat and yelled in his ear. "Jake!"

The announcer said, "We are experiencing difficulties with the video portion of our program due to technical problems which . . . which nobody understands. We hope to have everything in order for the Pittsburgh–San Diego kickoff. Stay tuned for the audio update."

Wilson was fuming at Wenger. "I told you not to use that!"

The veterinarian was offended. "I came here as a favor to a neighbor. As a rule, I don't make house calls."

"A fine time to start," moaned Link.

"That's uncalled for, Link," said Liz.

Wenger picked up his bag and made for the door. "I don't have to put up with this. And I don't intend to miss any more games!" With a huff, he stepped into the outer hall.

"Please, Doctor," pleaded Liz. She followed him. "They're new cat owners." She left the door ajar. They could be heard down the hall. Wilson frantically tried to revive Jake.

"It's *me*, Jake! Jake!"

But the cat didn't budge. The enormity of the situation dawned on Link.

"We're finished, Frank," he cried. "He's blotto!"

"Look on the bright side. San Diego could still win!" replied Wilson.

"Yeah, and San Diego could still lose!" yelled Link. "And where does that leave this little guy?" He nodded toward Jake. "He's blown his rendezvous. *And* my fifteen hundred clams!"

Furious, Liz stalked back in.

"That was absolutely uncalled for, Frank!"

"Liz, butt out," said Wilson.

"What?"

"Cancel the bet!" Wilson told Link. "Call Ernie!"

Link rushed to the phone and began dialing. "He'll never buy it."

Wilson frantically tried to revive the cat. "Jake! We've got *problems!* Jake! Speak to me!"

"Is everyone crazy?" cried Liz.

Link said, "Line's busy! We'll never get through —he's taking bets!"

"We'd better get down there!" said Wilson.

"Like yesterday!" Link slammed the phone on the cradle and rushed toward the door. Jake in his arms, Wilson followed.

"Now just a minute . . ." began Liz. She was alone. She followed.

"I would like—no, I *demand* an explanation!" she said as they moved toward the elevator. "What's going on?"

"Later, Liz," said Wilson.

She blocked the elevator door when it opened. "No, *now*," she said.

Link anxiously glanced at his watch. "We've got exactly six minutes before that game starts."

"Liz . . ." Wilson appealed.

"I'm not moving till you explain," she said firmly.

"Okay, okay, in the elevator." They stepped in and the door closed behind them.

Moments later, in the lobby, it slid open. And Liz's face was ashen.

"Outer space?" she cried. "Are you putting me on, Frank Wilson?"

Wilson pulled her out of the lobby. "Tell you the whole story in the car."

Moving toward the Volksie, Wilson made his explanation. Liz stopped. Not once—several times. The story was too much to expect. She turned from Link to Wilson to Link to Wilson. *Both* couldn't be nuts. They were in Wilson's Beetle and on their way when she began to believe. The car shot away from the curb.

One block behind them, the driver of a pink and baby blue panel truck turned on the ignition. The logo on its side read: STORK DYDEE SERVICE. Its trademark was a smiling stork flying a happy baby tucked in a diaper. Two tough-looking men sat in the front seat of the truck. They wore appropriate logos on their pink and baby blue uniforms. Their jackets bulged with firearms.

"That's them," said one of the Dydee men. "Get going."

The truck began to make a U turn but was blocked by an elderly lady pedaling her grocery-laden tricycle.

Nearby, on the front lawn of the apartment house, a policeman was questioning Stallwood. He was holding Rupert's camera as the two sisters looked on. They were making low clucking noises that made no sense.

"Now let me understand this," said the cop. "You were photographing nuthatches from their ledge?" He nodded toward the women.

116

"It's their molting season," explained Stallwood.

The cop was dubious.

"One way to find out," he said. "Check the film."

The game was up. Stallwood panicked, seized the camera, and ran, leaping over the hedge and toward the sidewalk. The policeman, three steps behind, tripped over the hedge as Stallwood cut toward the corner.

A six-year-old boy was crouching alongside his skateboard, making an adjustment to a wheel. Without losing stride, Stallwood hopped onto the skateboard and spun down the sidewalk. The cop was ten yards behind. The skateboard, Stallwood still astride, hopped over the curb at a corner. The Dydee truck spun around the corner, swerved to avoid hitting Stallwood, and screeched to a halt. The abrupt stop jerked the back doors of the truck open to reveal a massive automatic machine gun, its barrel pointing directly at the cop. He raised his arms.

"An armed Dydee truck!" he gasped.

Two Dydee guards were crouched behind the automatic weapon. One flashed his I.D. card.

"Military intelligence!" he cried.

He slammed the doors shut and the Dydee truck whirled away in pursuit of Wilson. His arms still in the air, the cop looked after it with incredulity. Up dashed the six-year-old boy.

"I want to report a stolen skateboard!" he said.

Wilson had the accelerator pressed to the floor. The Dydee truck was thirty yards behind, and directly on its tail were two Hell's Angels types riding tandem on their motorcycles. Wilson stopped short for a traffic light. The Dydee truck squealed to a stop and its back doors flew open. There was the machine gun, ready to blast away. Wide-eyed, the Hell's Angels made an abrupt U turn and screamed out of sight.

Alongside the driver, a Dydee guard spoke with hushed tones into a radio transmitter.

"Dydee One calling Hopscotch. Come in, Hopscotch."

Stilton's voice was heard. "This is Sequoia. Go ahead, Dydee One."

"General, we have the subject in sight," said the guard. "Also that garbage expert and the dame from the car pool. And an unconscious cat."

"A *what?*" asked Stilton.

"A cat, sir!"

"Never mind the cat! Just don't let the others out of your sight!" ordered the general.

Wilson's car pulled up to Ernie's pool hall. It ran the length of the second floor of an aging graffiti-scrolled building in a squalid section of the town. An aged arrow pointed up the rickety stairs.

"They've just stopped," the Dydee guard said into the transmitter. "They're going into Earnest Ernie's. Looks like a Mafia tie-in, General."

The general faced ERL's director. "What kind of a zoo are you running down there, Heffel?"

Link tore up the stairway, followed by Liz and Wilson, the cat in his arms. The Dydee truck parked discreetly down the street.

The room smelled of smoke and disinfectant. In the far corner of the pool hall, Sarasota Slim was practicing. With unerring precision, one ball after another dropped into pockets. Earnest Ernie was checking the day's receipts while Weasel and Honest Harry crouched in front of a blacked-out TV set. They listened attentively to the announcer. A few disreputable types shot pool while one loafer chomped on a large submarine sandwich overflowing with onions and peppers. Link rushed in.

"Ernie . . ." cried Link.

Ernie glanced up. "Well, look who's here."

"I want to cancel my Chargers bet!"

In mock surprise, Ernie said, "Cancel your Chargers bet? Now I wonder why!"

"Playing a hunch, Ernie!"

"Not a bad hunch, Link, with San Diego ten points behind," said Ernie. Wilson and Liz drew up.

"Already?" Wilson asked.

"*Seventeen*, boss!" yelled Weasel. "Steelers scored another one!"

"There goes our hundred and twenty!" moaned the physicist.

"I'm the one who should be crying!" said Link. "Fifteen hundred bucks of that . . ."

"Can't you do *something?*" Liz interrupted.

"With him out cold?" Wilson said, peering into the cat's face. The cat was tucked in the physicist's arms. Wilson shook him slightly, to wake him. "We need you, Jake! Wake up!"

There was no response.

"Is he breathing?" asked Link. Wilson placed an ear next to the cat's nostrils.

"Snoring," said Wilson.

"Can't you bet on something else?" Liz asked.

Wilson's eyes lit. "Now you're talking. Basketball. Who's playing?"

Link said, "Philadelphia and Boston."

"Great."

"Next Tuesday," said Link. Wilson moved toward Ernie.

"Ernie, is there a hockey game we can bet on?"

The man shook his head. "Sorry."

Wilson turned to Link. "Horse race? Boxing? Demolition derby? Anything to get even?"

Ernie said slyly, "If you guys really want some action, there's Sarasota Slim."

"Who's Sarasota Slim?" asked Wilson.

"He indulges occasionally in a friendly game of pool with a small wager on the side," said Ernie.

"Nothing doing!" cried Link.

"Why not?" asked Wilson.

"Sarasota Slim's a *hustler*, Wilson!"

Wilson moved back to Ernie. "You've got yourself a bet, Ernie."

"Are you nuts?" Link cried. "That guy can make a pool ball sit up and talk!"

Wilson drew Link aside. "Yes, but *we've* got the . . . uh . . ." Surreptitiously, he indicated Jake's collar.

"What good is it? Jake's blotto," whispered Link.

"You don't understand. I know how to use it. Jake taught me. To repair the spaceship."

"He taught *you?* To repair . . . ?"

"You think you can?" interrupted Liz.

"Do we have a choice?" asked Wilson. He turned to Ernie. "Okay, Ernie, what's the odds?"

"You against Sarasota Slim?" There was a wisp of a smile on Ernie's face. Another sucker.

"Wait a minute, Frank . . ." said Link.

Ernie interrupted. "Because you deserve a chance to break even, and because I like your style, eight to one."

"That's all? Suppose Link plays?"

"Link plays?" Ernie pondered. "Considerin' the shape he's in, ten to one."

"How . . . how about the lady?"

Liz was startled. *"Me?"*

Ernie looked her over, beginning with her ankles and working up.

"For the lady, twenty to one," he replied.

"I can't even hold the pole, Frank!" Liz protested.

"Are you bananas?" Link asked him.

121

Wilson corralled his little group into a confidential knot and whispered hoarsely.

"I'm desperate, is what I am! No money, no gold. No gold, no lift-off. But if we deliver, look what we get in return. The solution to half of this planet's problems."

Liz reflected, then said soberly, "Just show me which end to hold."

"Good girl," said Wilson. "Now we need a stake." He dug into his pants pocket. "I've got twelve bucks."

"I've got twenty," said Link. He withdrew his wallet and handed a twenty-dollar bill to Wilson.

"Liz?" asked Wilson.

She opened her purse reluctantly.

"All I have is my mad money," she said.

"Let me have it," said Wilson.

She withdrew a wad of greenbacks, hesitated, then gave them to Frank. Wilson counted the bills.

"Four hundred and eighty bucks!" he cried.

"This dame gets mad," Link said.

Her expression wasn't a happy one. "I was going to buy a whole spring wardrobe."

Wilson ignored her. "That gives us five hundred and twelve."

A crowd gathered, sensing the forthcoming drama. Sarasota Slim eased into the picture. Directly behind him was the man eating the long submarine sandwich. Wilson plunked three hundred dollars into Ernie's hands.

"Three hundred at twenty to one!"

Link jerked the three hundred out of Ernie's wet palms.

"Not in your lifetime, Frank!" he cried. "You crazy? *Honest Harry* holds!"

He slapped the three hundred into Honest Harry's waiting mitt and Ernie matched the bet.

"You want Honest Harry?" he said. "You got Honest Harry."

As Honest Harry audibly counted the stake, Wilson surreptitiously removed Jake's collar.

"Sixty-three hundred, and may the best man win. Or woman. As the case may be. Break," said Honest Harry.

Link whispered to Wilson, "Maybe we should think a minute. Maybe there's another way out."

"Another Pittsburgh touchdown, boss!" cried Weasel.

"Break!" said Link.

Wilson slipped Jake into Link's arms. "Keep your eye on him," he said in a low voice. "If he just blinks *once* . . ." The physicist, clutching the collar, moved aside.

Link sniffed. He smelled onions. He turned and stared into the friendly face of the moustached submarine sandwich eater, who looked up at Link. A friendly soul.

"Hi," the man beamed.

The onion concentrate wafted upward. Link flinched and his eyes almost double-crossed. He stepped away.

Wilson handed Liz the cue stick. Smirking

viewers stood a respectful distance from the table and began nudging each other. This was too good to miss. Liz was holding her cue as if it were a golf club. The onlookers chuckled.

Sarasota Slim said, "Excuse me, lady, if I may be so bold."

Magnanimously, he corrected her grip, then her stance. Now she held the stick as if it were an ice pick. Her face told the story—she was scared. Sarasota Slim chewed on his toothpick. A cinch, said his expression.

"Your break, Miss," he said.

She approached the table and froze. "What do I do?" she asked Wilson.

"Help her, Link," Wilson said.

"The object of the game, Liz, is to get all those balls in the pockets," Link told her. "You hit *this* ball, called the cue ball, with the *cue stick*. The thing in your hands. The cue ball then hits the pack, up there. You're gonna do fine, Liz, stop worrying, half the battle's mental."

"That's my problem," she said.

Liz made one last silent appeal to Wilson. He reassured her with a nod of the head as Ernie smugly rocked back and forth on his heels. Oh, if there were only more days like this.

Elizabeth bent to take aim and the collar in Wilson's hand began to flicker. In a wild, desperate motion, Liz let the stick fly. The cue ball bounced off the table, skipped hippity-hop from one table to the next, whipped a cigar out of a man's mouth, knocked someone's hat off, bowled a beer bottle off a tray, completed the circuit of the whole room, and landed back on the home table. The pack broke up. Not one ball rolled into a pocket.

There was no expression on Sarasota's face as he calmly stepped forward. He was in no rush. He studied the layout, then bent over, and bam, bam, bam, put every ball away. Honest Harry handed Earnest Ernie the winnings. He counted the bills methodically.

In another secret confab with Link and Wilson, Liz said, "It's hopeless!"

"We need Jake," said Link.

"How is he?" asked Wilson.

"Sleeping like a kitten," replied Link.

Ernie yelled over. "Well, gentlemen, you had enough?"

"No," said Wilson. "Providing you up the odds."

Link protested, "Frank!"

"You have any other suggestions?" Wilson asked. "How about it, Ernie?"

Ernie said, "I really don't think the little lady should play."

"We'll decide that. What odds, Ernie?"

Ernie studied Liz again. This time from top to bottom, then up again. "Seein' as how she has a lot of moxie, thirty to one."

"Thirty to one! That's larceny, Ernie! You saw how she played!" cried Wilson.

Honest Harry interrupted. "Thirty to one does seem like a short price for a lady who is operating under certain deficiencies. Like no talent."

Ernie became magnanimous. "Okay, fifty to one."

"A hundred and fifty at fifty to one!" cried Wilson, and slipped Honest Harry seven twenties and a ten.

"How much do we have left?" asked Link, uneasily.

"Please, Link," Wilson reassured him.

The slob eating the sandwich sidled up to Link as Ernie covered Wilson's bet. Link didn't have to sniff to know who was standing beside him. He turned his head wearily and peered down. Yep. Blowing up in his face.

"Hi," said the muncher.

This one not only smelled of onions, but peppers. Link's knees almost buckled. He felt ill, tried to swallow, but couldn't. He placed Jake on a chair and walked to the water fountain. The muncher took another bite. He'd had enough. He rubbed his mouth with a coat sleeve, dropped the remains of the sandwich on the chair, and moved toward the pool table. Jake's eyes began to quiver. Then to blink. One eye opened. An inch away from his nose was a sandwich. Onions, peppers. . . . His eyes began to tear.

Elizabeth cast an anxious glance at Wilson as she edged up to the pool table.

"Your break, Miss," said Sarasota.

Wilson's gesture reinforced her. "Don't worry," it seemed to say. "This time we do it." She managed a brave smile, leaned over, and whacked the cue ball. Taking off like a low-flying jet, it hit the front wall, then caromed off wall after wall. Spectators and players flattened themselves on the floor as the ball whistled overhead. Up to the ceiling it went and plopped down. And sat still. It was lying on its home table, exactly where she had hit it a minute ago. Elizabeth, Wilson, and Link stared with incredulity.

Sarasota Slim shook a small finger in his ear as he appraised the situation. Then he broke the pack and five balls went into the pockets. One by one, he put the rest away.

Ernie was collecting his winnings when Liz first heard the cat. It was such a low meow, she wasn't certain. But when she turned, there he was, sitting on his haunches. Wild-eyed. His tail swirled. Cautiously, Liz tapped Wilson on the shoulder.

"You're not going to believe this," she whispered. He glanced at her and knew instantly.

"Meow," purred Jake. Joyfully, the three rushed toward him.

The physicist was placing the collar around the cat's neck when he propositioned Ernie.

"We bet the works! Sixty-two!" Wilson said.

"Your last monies, I can't do it," Ernie told him.

"The odds, Ernie!"

"It's not sportin'."

"Ernie!" cried Wilson.

"I happen to have principles!" began Ernie.

"You aren't going to give us a chance to win our money back?" cried Wilson.

"Okay, okay," said Ernie. "A hundred to one." Wilson deliberated.

"Suppose *she* gives Sarasota Slim twelve balls. *And* the break?" asked Wilson.

Laughter from the assembly. Even a trace of a smile on Sarasota Slim's thin lips.

Ernie beamed. "I like your sense of humor, kid. *Five hundred* to one!"

Wilson topped him, "How about blindfolded?"

The crowd became hysterical. Ernie was bent double with laughter. "Two thousand to one!" he managed.

"You're on!" cried Wilson.

The smile froze on Ernie's face. Wilson handed Honest Harry sixty-two dollars.

"Wait a minute, you don't mean it?" said Ernie.

"Of course I mean it—sixty-two bucks!"

"You seriously serious?" asked Ernie.

"You're not thinking of welching, are you?" asked Wilson.

Ernie growled, "Watch it, Buster."

Honest Harry said, "It would not do your reputation any credit if word was to circulate that you reneged on a wager duly offered and accepted, Ernie."

A bead of perspiration appeared on Ernie's

brow. He glanced at Wilson, then at Honest Harry, then back to Wilson. "Get the loot, Weasel," he said softly.

"That's over a hundred and twenty G's, boss!" Weasel said. He was worried.

"Get the loot!" repeated Ernie. Weasel began to say something, then thought better of it. He slipped away to get the cash. Link removed a handkerchief from his jacket and began tying it around Elizabeth's eyes.

Ernie interrupted. "Oh, no you don't. *I* tie."

He snatched a black muffler off a bystander's neck and tested it with his own eyes. Good. No one could see through that. He was winding the muffler around Liz's eyes when Weasel returned. The man was carrying one hundred and twenty-four thousand dollars in one-thousand-dollar bills, and he wasn't too happy about it.

"You sure, boss?" he asked.

Ernie took the bills and ordered Wilson's bet. "Your break, Slim," said Ernie.

Sarasota Slim nodded. His smile was confident, even cocky. He made a ceremony out of chalking his cue stick, then warmed his hands, made a little strut, and bent over to take aim. As he shot, the cue ball slipped aside three inches. The startled audience was witness to a first. Not only did Slim miss the cue ball, his stick ripped up the cloth. The hustler's jaw dropped. He glanced mournfully at Ernie. Ernie was seething.

A hush. It was the dame's turn. All eyes on the

table. An alert cat was tucked in Wilson's arms and no one noticed the glowing collar.

Elizabeth leaned over her cue stick.

"Go get 'em, baby," said Wilson.

She pulled her stick back.

"Fire!" cried Wilson.

The triangular pack split wide open upon the cue ball's impact, and every ball but one flew into pockets. This, the eight ball, rolled up on the rim of the table and made one complete circuit. Then it dropped back on the felt, edged up to a pocket, hesitated, then fell in. The table was bare. The crowd was stunned.

A whooping Wilson tore off Liz's blindfold and whirled her high in the air. Link danced with joy. Weasel and Sarasota Slim sat in a trauma while Ernie sobbed in a heap.

Chapter Ten

A cloud of cigar smoke curled up in the projector's light. In the darkened room, all that could be seen of the figure in the huge wing chair was a pair of sneakered feet. They rested on the floor while the head they belonged to seemed to be bent double, almost touching the carpeting.

It and all the other heads in the room. There were four in all. They were watching Stallwood's home movie on a flickering screen. The pictures he had taken were upside down.

Mister Olympus and his two beefy employees were seeing them for the first time in his sumptuous private office. The films were unedited. Just as Rupert Stallwood had shot them from Wilson's ledge. There was the beer pouring out of the can and into Link's face, then back again. The cat's collar glowing. There was Link getting rolled up in paper towels. Stallwood had caught it all, through Wilson's windows and parted drapes. All of it. Upside down.

Stallwood said, "Terribly sorry about this, Mister Olympus. I took these pictures at the risk of life and limb, sir."

From somewhere in the darkness an unctuous voice replied, "No need to apologize, friend."

"Amazing," said another voice.

"My sentiments precisely," said Stallwood.

The film was ended. Mister Olympus's hand reached out and pressed a button. The room lit up on a rheostat.

In size and decor, it was opulent. Flanking one whole wall was a massive wall-sized map of the world, a telecommunications panel, and a series of wall clocks. Mister Olympus knew the correct time, that very moment, in every major country in the world. He had operations in all of them.

A huge crescent desk dominated one end of the room. Beside it stood a bodyguard, Omar, a menacing, towering creature, alongside his companion, the evil-eyed hairless Choirmaster.

Mister Olympus rose from the depths of his chair. Surprisingly, he was a small man, wearing a well-tailored suit of soft leather. His dark hair was parted in the middle, plastered down, while a small pencil-thin moustache graced his upper lip. The man's voice, almost a purr, masked an iron will of total self-control. He was a person who was accustomed to obedience.

Omar stepped to the bar-kitchen area to pour tea.

"Mister Olympus said quietly, "If I didn't see it with my own eyes . . ."

"Absolutely extraordinary, Mister Olympus," said Choirmaster. His boss ignored him.

"Didn't I tell you?" said Stallwood ecstatically.

Napoleonlike, Olympus strode to his desk. Omar presented him with a cup of tea.

"Thank you, Omar. Would anyone else care for some rose hip tea?" Olympus made these gestures of hospitality occasionally, expecting no acceptances.

"I'd love tea, sir," said Stallwood. "How do you make yours? I find that if you steep the leaves with sassafras . . ." He broke off. The three were glaring at him.

"Pour the gentleman his tea, Omar," said Olympus with an edge. Omar peered down at Stallwood with menace, then faded into the background. Silence, broken only by the spoon tinkling in Olympus's teacup.

"Yes, you have described it with accuracy, Choirmaster," Olympus said after a time. "It is extraordinary. Incredible."

"Yes sir," said Choirmaster.

"I see infinite possibilities, a *revolution* in transportation! *Space* exploration, *industrialization* of the planets. . . ." His eyes were kindled. He rose and began to pace. "And the most interesting aspect of all, the *economics*. The leverage I've been waiting for, Choirmaster. The man who owns that collar can control . . ."

"The world!" interrupted Choirmaster.

"The universe!" cried Olympus. He was not to be topped.

"My thoughts exactly, sir," beamed Stallwood. Olympus clenched his fist and smashed it on the desk. Omar slipped Stallwood his cup of tea.

"So happy to have played a role, sir," bubbled Stallwood. "Could well call for a bonus, wouldn't you say, sir?"

"No, I wouldn't!" snarled Olympus. He looked at Stallwood with amazement. The impudence of the man. Omar and Choirmaster instinctively moved in toward Stallwood, whose teacup began to rattle.

"Just a wee . . . tiny . . . ?" He smiled uncomfortably.

"Do you *have* the collar, Stallwood?" barked Olympus.

"Have it, sir? Me, sir? No, sir."

"Well, until you do, don't talk about bonuses. Until that collar is in my possession—"

"Oh, I'll get it for you, sir, depend on it, sir!"

"I want that collar and I want it now!"

"And now you shall have it, sir!"

"Not *you*, bumblebrain!" cried Olympus. "Prepare the copter, Choirmaster, I'm taking charge myself!"

The Hopscotch operation was moving in high gear. Experts and technicians swarmed through the hangar and in and out of the mobile computer trailers. The machines themselves buzzed and made clickety-clack noises as banks of colored lights flicked on and off. It was all very reassuring.

General Stilton, flanked by *his* aides and Doctor Heffel, hovered over an expected printout. Information was being fed the monster.

"All set, General," said the technician in charge. "Fully programmed. With all relevant information. Question number one, sir."

This was the big moment. The general stood tall. "*Ask her who the pilot is,*" he ordered.

The technician pressed several buttons. The machine tapped a printout on its monitor. The message read: IT'S A CAT.

The general was infuriated.

"It's a cat?" he stormed. He kicked the machine. "You call yourself a computer? Get on the ball, soldier! Feed that information through again! Reassess!"

The technician cried, "Yes, sir!" Several others went to his assistance as Captain Anderson came on the run.

"General Stilton, sir!" he exclaimed.

"What is it, Captain?" the general said impatiently.

"That purchase Doctor Link made late this afternoon . . . we've checked it out, sir! It was a large quantity of gold, sir!"

"Gold!" screamed the general. "It's a Machiavellian conspiracy!" He seized the radio and spoke into it. "Where are you, Dydee One?"

"Outside the suspect's apartment," replied Dydee One.

"Don't let those scum out of your sight!"

The computer was spewing another printout.

"Another printout, General!" cried the technician.

The general snapped off the sheet of paper and read: DEFINITELY A CAT!

"Of all the . . . wait a minute." The general grabbed the radio. "Dydee One, didn't they carry a cat into that pool hall?!"

"Yes, sir, they did," was the reply.

The general released the radio. "That does it! Gentlemen, it's time to move in!"

He snapped his riding crop and strode out.

All hands were active in Wilson's apartment. There was little time to spare before Jake's departure. A large bar of gold rested on a table while in the kitchen Liz packed a picnic basket. Things she thought Jake would like on his trip. Only Jake appeared to be calm. He was snuggled up to Lucy Belle and occasionally glanced up to dictate notes to Wilson and Link. They tried to make sense of his equations.

Liz said, "I've packed a nice basket for your trip back, Jake. Something to remember us by."

"Lots of that gorgeous tuna, I hope," said Jake.

"Better believe it," she said.

Wilson said, "Listen, Jake, I didn't get all that formula for Orn three. What comes after EMC squared to the seventh power, three times the quadrant of HC minus . . ."

"Plus 0 to the fourth oogle, minus the sum of the unstable elements," Jake told him. "What else you packing, Liz?"

"Some of that chopped liver."

"Beautiful."

Link was admiring the bar of gold.

"One hundred and twenty thousand dollars in one lump sum! Man!" exclaimed Link. "Tell you what, Jake. How'd you like to hang around a few days and watch me parlay this into real dough."

"Dough?"

"Bread," explained Link.

"Sorry, Link," said Jake. "How we doin' for time, Frank? Lift-off is dawn minus zero, on the nose."

Liz glanced at her watch. "Oh, oh. You'd better be leaving."

"All good things must come to an end," said the cat. He rose and glanced at Lucy Belle. "Hate to say goodbye, doll."

Lucy Belle meowed.

"I'll miss you too, honey," said Jake. He nuzzled her. "You have one sweet set of whiskers."

"You'll be late, Jake!" warned Liz.

"Yeah . . . well . . ." Reluctantly, he left Lucy Belle and hopped onto the table beside the gold bar. "Time to reduce it," he said.

"Reduce it?" Liz was puzzled.

Link said, "What're you talking about?"

"Didn't he tell you?" said Wilson. "They extrapolate inversely calculating the mass. It's in the notes here." He flicked through his notepad. "They use a system based on the lingle content rather than . . ."

Jake interrupted. "You've got a whole lifetime to explain, Frank. I've got less than an hour, so if everybody will stand back . . ."

He faced the gold and was taking a deep breath when the door burst open. In rushed General Stilton and three aides. The sergeant wielded a carbine as if he meant business.

"Don't move!" stormed the general. "All hands in the air!"

All but Jake complied.

Wilson said, "Who the . . . ?"

"*Doctor Frank Wilson?*" barked the general.

"What *is* this? You can't break in like . . ." began Wilson.

"*Doctor Frank Wilson,*" cried the general. "*You are under arrest!*"

"And the pussycat, General!" said the colonel.

"And the pussycat, General!" cried Stilton. "Colonel, read their rights to them!"

"Captain!" cried the colonel.

"*Ser---geant!*" bellowed the captain.

The general interrupted. "Never mind! You have the right to remain silent! Anything you say will be used against you in a court of law! You have the right to . . ."

Zap! Jake's glowing collar froze the general in mid-passage. His three aides were immobile.

Liz gasped. "Good heavens!"

"What happened?" Link cried.

"They're frozen," said Wilson.

"Holy mackerel!" Link said. "Pentagon popsicles!"

"They're on to us, Jake," said Wilson. "How we getting into Hopscotch? You can't zap the whole base."

"I'll think of something," Jake replied.

"The whole place will be on alert!" cried Wilson.

"You mind if I get this gold reduced first?" asked Jake. He turned to face the gold bar and inhaled deeply. "Everybody back!"

They moved.

Jake concentrated. In a flash of tremendous power, the gold began to sizzle, then condense. It became a tiny unit. Smoke curled from his collar as Jake shook off the effects. His paw wiped his brow.

In awe, Wilson exclaimed. "Unbelievable!"

"Are you all right, Jake?" Liz asked anxiously.

"I think so" was the weak reply. "Let's move, Frank."

"Wait a second," said Wilson. His finger was poised in the air. He had an idea. "I know how to get into the base."

"How?" Liz asked.

"Right there. Staring right at us. *Him*." Wilson jerked his thumb toward the frozen general.

Stilton had parked his command car directly in front of Wilson's apartment building and had the Dydee truck stationed some distance away, facing the command car. Nearby were two jeeps.

A Dydee guard glanced at his wristwatch. "They should be coming out with those prisoners. I'll turn this thing around."

The truck moved up to a ramp, then reversed.

A long, sleek black limousine came slowly into sight. Omar, in a chauffeur's uniform, drove cautiously. In the sumptuously outfitted rear section sat Olympus, enthroned. Stallwood and Choirmaster faced him on the jump seats.

Stallwood peered out. "What's the military doing here?"

"Looks like complications," said Choirmaster.

"I *thrive* on complications," said Olympus.

The Dydee truck pulled back, directly in front of the limo, then stopped with a jerk. The rear doors swung open and there, in Omar's face, was the machine gun.

"Uh oh," muttered Stallwood. He had no stomach for weapons. Especially those directed at him. One guard in the rear of the Dydee truck scrambled to his feet and whipped the doors shut.

"Looks like *exceptional* complications," said Stallwood.

"I *thrive* on exceptional complications," said Olympus.

Upstairs, in Wilson's apartment, Wilson was outfitting himself with components of the general's uniform. Stilton had been stripped to his paisley shorts.

"How do I look?" asked Wilson.

"In another ten years, you'll grow into them," Link replied.

Wilson adjusted the general's wraparound glasses over his eyes.

"Yes or no?" asked Wilson.

"Yes. It's not great, but it'll work," said Link.

"You really look commanding, Frank," Liz said proudly.

"Okay—with luck, this should get us on the base," said Wilson. He peered at his watch. "Fifty-three minutes to lift-off, let's get out of here!"

He swooped Jake in his arms. "I'm depending on you, Frank," said the animal. Liz barred the way. She spoke tenderly to Jake and stroked his chin. He liked it.

"Case things get fouled up and we don't see you again, Jake . . ."

"Come on!" Wilson cried impatiently. "You can say your goodbyes on the way down." Link was the last to leave. He had taken a moment to face the frozen general.

"This almost makes up for what I went through in Korea!" he said. Then left.

In the limousine, Stallwood was still bemoaning his luck.

"A fine time for the Army to move in!" he said.

Omar said, "Do we leave, Mister Olympus?"

"We will leave when I say so," said Olympus.

The front-seat Dydee truck guard was becoming impatient. "Maybe we ought to give them a buzz." The driver nodded. His assistants picked up the transmitter. "Dydee One calling Big Cheese . . ."

"Sequoia, not Big Cheese," his buddy corrected.

"Code words changed for this operation. Come in, Big Cheese. Come in. Dydee One calling Big Cheese . . ."

The driver nudged him. "Here comes General Cheese—I mean, Stilton."

Wilson, in Stilton's uniform with the brim of his cap pulled down, moved briskly to the command car. Jake was snug in his arms. Liz and Link flanked him. The Dydee truck guards appeared puzzled.

Stallwood pointed. "There's the cat! The general has the cat!"

Choirmaster said, "So long, ball game."

"I will not brook pessimism!" ordered Olympus. "Do I make myself clear?"

The driver of the truck stepped out. He wanted

a better view. There was something funny going on. He could smell it.

"Where's the general going?" his assistant asked.

"*That's* the general?" asked the driver.

"It's not?"

They looked at each other, reacting in alarm. The driver pounded on the rear paneling of the truck.

"Trouble! Open those doors!" He and his buddy seized weapons. The guard detail in the rear began rattling the back doors. Normally, they opened too soon. Now they wouldn't open at all.

Wilson placed Jake on the dashboard and switched on the ignition. Liz and Link were swept aside as the Dydee guards approached on the run.

"Halt! In the name of the U.S. Army!" barked a guard.

The guards in the rear of the truck bashed open the rear doors and swung the machine gun into position.

"Oh, boy!" cried Wilson. "Do your thing, Jake!"

The cat's collar glowed. Zap. In mid-step, the guard and the driver were frozen. Their buddies behind the machine gun were as still as statues. Powerless.

Olympus saw it all. His mouth was agape. "Fantastic!" he cried.

"You see?" said Stallwood. "Just as I told you, sir!"

"I must have that cat," cried Olympus. *"I will have that cat!"*

"I'd volunteer, sir, but you saw what he did to those men," said Stallwood.

Wilson waved to Link and Liz, who was holding Lucy Belle close to Jake.

"Good luck!" cried Link.

"Take care!" said Liz. Lucy Belle meowed as Jake gave her one last melting look.

Wilson yelled, "Let's go!" and the command car shot away.

"They're leaving, sir!" cried Stallwood.

Choirmaster said, "They're escaping!"

"If you have any hopes of getting that cat, sir, I'd advise . . ." began Stallwood.

"No need to rush, gentlemen," replied Olympus. He tapped Omar on the shoulder. "They've left something very valuable behind." The giant slipped the automatic revolver out of his holster and stepped out of the car. Olympus nodded toward Liz and Link. The gun held firmly, Omar stepped forward. The man and the woman reacted in astonishment, then fear.

At Hopscotch, the general's command car screeched to a halt. Out of the guard hut popped an officer. Beside him stood a corporal with a clipboard. Both saluted. The salutes were returned.

The officer peered into the car. "General Stilton?" he asked.

"Of course!" was the bark.

"Of course, sir!" replied the officer, pulling back. "I'll sign you in, sir!" The corporal gave him the clipboard and the officer began to scribble.

"General Stilton and . . . cat. Is the cat cleared, sir?"

"What do *you* think?"

"Sorry, sir!"

"I want all personnel out of the hangar! Immediately! We're moving the ship!" ordered Wilson.

"But sir," said the officer. "If we ordered them out of the hangar, how will . . ."

"Soldier!" thundered Wilson.

"Out of the hangar, sir! Immediately, sir!"

The command car roared off and the officer doubled back into the hut, almost knocking over his corporal.

"Look where you're going, soldier!" shouted the officer.

"Yes, sir!" replied the corporal.

The officer picked up the phone and jiggled the receiver frantically.

The officer barked into the phone. "All personnel out of the hangar! On the double. . . . General Stilton, that's who the heck who!"

146

The command car swept into the hangar. Jake's collar began to glow.

In Wilson's apartment, time had expired. Jake's zap had worn off and the general and his aides were unfrozen. Stilton resumed his conversation where he had left off.

". . . talk to a lawyer and have him present while you are questioned!" ordered Stilton. "If you cannot afford to . . ."

He glanced around. Where was Wilson? Where was the garbage expert? The woman? The cat? He looked down. He was stripped of everything but his shorts. The general blew up like Vesuvius.

"Colonel!"

Colonel Woodruff glanced at his superior, then saw the general's shorts. He got the message. He began undressing. Post haste.

"Captain!" he ordered.

The captain moved instinctively, swiftly, dropping his pants as he jerked off his jacket.

"Ser---geant!" he screamed. The colonel shoved his clothes to the general while the captain tossed his toward the colonel. They dressed while undressing.

Sergeant Duffy knew what the end result would be, and who would wind up without clothes. Musical chairs. He whipped off his apparel and as fast as they came off the captain seized them. The clothing didn't fit his superiors, but at least they wore *something*.

He wound up with shorts, shoes, socks, and an undershirt embossed with the words GO NAVY.

The massive doors at the hangar began to open, ponderously. The spaceship edged slowly out to the tarmac. It stopped near the cat.

"Time?" asked Jake.

"One thirty to countdown," Wilson replied.

"Close," said Jake. A ramp emerged from the ship and Wilson and Jake rushed up into the cabin.

Jake cried, "Insert the gold in the microtransformer!"

Wilson withdrew the gold pellet from his inner pocket. It was in an envelope. He slid it into the slot and the artichoke began to accelerate, whirl, then rise. Now the ship was humming. Radiating. Elements on the console began blinking.

"Good," said Jake. "Let's see if we have contact. Zunar Five Jay calling Mother Ship," he spoke into the console. "Come in, Mother . . ."

"Hi there, fella," replied the mother ship voice. "See you made it with nothing to spare."

"Tell me about it," Jake said sarcastically.

"We are one zero five to lift-off. Come in on Ray zero three nine two. Adjust transmuter."

"Transmuter adjusted," said Jake.

"Countdown starts at twenty. Set clonometer."

"Clonometer set. Give me a printout, please," said Jake.

The light-hearted reply came in a singsong. "Coming your way, without de-lay."

Wilson was in awe. "That's another cat?"

"From meow to tail," replied Jake.

The computers began to clickety-clack.

The long black limousine curled up to the front gate at Hopscotch, slowed up to deposit a passenger. Link was shoved out and the sedan disappeared. The garbage expert ran toward the guard hut.

"I've got to get to that spaceship! Right away!" cried Link.

"Who are you?" inquired the puzzled officer.

"A friend of Frank Wilson's! . . . General Stilton's, I mean!"

The real General Stilton, at that very moment, was dashing out of Wilson's apartment building with his aides directly behind him. Stilton was in a fury and had every right to be. It was bad enough that the cat was gone, and Wilson, and the others, but he was busting his seams in an absurd uniform. Sporting *colonel's* wings. He glanced about. The Dydee guards were frozen and his car was gone! The general thundered to the heavens.

"Call the police!" he stormed.

At Hopscotch, the officer took no chances. He drove Link to the hangar in his jeep personally. He didn't know what to make of this character, but a lot of strange things were going on tonight and it was best to be sure.

The spaceship was firing up. Before the jeep

even stopped, Link was out and running toward the craft. The officer brought his jeep to a halt and dashed after him.

"Wilson!" cried Link. "It's me! Hey, Wilson!"

Wilson poked his head out of the ship's cabin.

"General!" cried the officer, "This man says . . ." Then he stopped. Wilson had his glasses off. "Hey, you're not the . . ."

Zap. He was frozen.

"Coming up on countdown!" said a voice from the mother ship.

Wilson cried, "What're you doing here, Link? Where's Liz?"

"Frank, it's a nightmare! Liz has been captured by Stallwood!"

"Have you been hitting the beer?" cried Wilson. "Stallwood of supplies and purchasing?"

"He's an agent! For a guy named Olympus! A power-crazy mogul who. . . . Frank, he's holding her for ransom!"

"For ransom?!"

"It's the collar or Liz!" yelled Link.

Wilson leaped from the ramp.

"They're out of their minds!" he cried. Jake made his appearance.

He cried, "I'm going with you, Frank!"

"Oh, no you're not! You've got your own problem, Jake! You want to get stuck on earth? You've got a responsibility to your mission!"

Jake cried, "But I'm the reason for the mess they're in!"

"All systems go!" said the mother ship voice. "Twenty seconds."

"Where is she?" Wilson asked Link.

"In Olympus's copter! At Dailey's Airport!"

"Let's go!"

"You're now off manual," said the mother ship voice. "Fifteen seconds. Locked in green. We have you on automatic."

"Frank . . ." wailed Jake.

"Jake, you're going home! Goodbye, friend!"

He ran toward the command car, hopped into the front seat, and started the motor. Link was right beside him. Behind, somewhere, he could hear the whooshing and the intensified roar. The ship was ready for lift-off.

"Ten seconds . . . nine . . . eight . . ." continued the voice.

The landing gear was raised and the sound became deafening.

". . . four . . . three . . . two . . . *lift-off!*"

Wilson and Link followed the rise of the craft.

"So long, Jake!" cried Wilson.

"Drop us a card!" yelled Link.

A voice said, "Okay, you clowns, let's move it!" It was Jake, heading toward them. One leap and he was in the back seat.

"Let's go!" he cried.

"You're one cat in a million!" cried Link.

Wilson said, "Jake, you're insane. You're here forever. On earth."

"You're wasting time, Wilson!" cried Jake. "The airport!"

The car took off and roared past the guard house. The corporal was there with his clipboard.

"Checking out!" cried Wilson. "General, cat, and guest!"

The corporal saluted as the sedan disappeared.

A convoy of three police cars, sirens screaming, rushed the general and his aides toward Hopscotch.

"Faster!" screamed the general.

"General! Look!" cried Colonel Woodruff.

He pointed in the distance. With awe, they viewed the spaceship rising.

"Stop this car!" cried the general. All four cars screamed to a halt. Stilton couldn't believe what he was seeing. The cat, Wilson—now they were all gone. His mission was a failure!

"I don't believe it!" he moaned. The spaceship disappeared in the sky.

"General!" cried the colonel. He was pointing ahead, down the highway. Stilton's command car whistled by, heading in the opposite direction.

"Wilson and the cat!" cried the captain.

"And the garbage expert!" added the colonel.

"Turn this thing around!" screamed the general.

Dawn was breaking when the command car, with Wilson at the wheel, whipped into the small Mom and Pop airfield known as Dailey's Airport.

Olympus's copter could be seen poised at the far end of a deserted runway. No other planes were on the field, but near an aged hangar was a dilapidated biplane, obviously once a Duster. It had no motor, no prop, and one wheel. The wings and the skin of the fuselage hung in strips. Obviously, the Stearman Duster was undergoing reconditioning. Parts of it were rusting on the ground, alongside tools. Its skeletal frame lay exposed, supported by makeshift carpentry.

Omar was at the controls of Olympus's luxurious executive copter. Choirmaster and Stallwood had tied Elizabeth's hands and were holding her and Lucy Belle.

"Here comes a car!" cried Choirmaster. He pointed at the window. Olympus put the binoculars to his eyes.

"It's the general's command car!" cried Stallwood. "I suggest we leave, sir!"

"Are you mad? The cat's in it with Wilson and Link!" cried Olympus.

"I suggest we stay, sir!" cried Stallwood.

"I knew he'd come to me," purred Olympus. He could almost taste it, the world was *his*.

"What's that?!" cried Choirmaster. He was pointing in another direction. Sirens could be heard. Over the crest of a hill, bordering the airport, came four police cars. Olympus trained his binoculars on them.

"It's the police!" cried Choirmaster.

"I suggest we leave, sir!" said Stallwood.

"The fools!" thundered Olympus. "Get this copter airborne! *Omar!*"

The machine swept up into the air and over the command car. Wilson made a U turn to follow, but the copter was gone. He stopped the car and the three passengers got out and gazed skyward.

"Olympus has them!" moaned Wilson.

Jake sized up the airport. "What kind of airport is this? Where are the planes?"

He spotted the Duster and scrambled toward it.

"You can't fly that, Jake!" Wilson yelled. "It has no propeller!"

But Jake was in the exposed cockpit and the plane was moving. His collar was glowing.

"You coming or staying?" cried Jake.

Wilson leaped for the cockpit and was half in and half out as the Stearman picked up speed.

"Hey, wait, you guys!" cried Link, dashing after them. But they were gone.

The manager of the airport scrambled out of his makeshift office. What was going on? He stared incredulously as the Duster staggered into the air. He blinked his eyes. The darned thing really *was* airborne. In fact, it was gaining altitude. He turned when he heard the sirens. Four police cars screamed to a halt and a general and aides dashed out of one. The general was furious. He waved his fists at the plane, fast disappearing after the copter.

"I want an all-Western-area scramble!" screamed the general.

In the copter, Omar glanced back. "We're being followed, sir!" Olympus turned. Behind them, several thousand yards, was a ridiculous-looking Duster. He brought his binoculars to his eyes.

"It's the cat and Wilson!" he cried.

"Now you're going to be sorry," said Elizabeth.

"*Am I?* Your boyfriend's going to pay for this," snarled Olympus.

Link had been seized and the general was questioning him. He bore in.

"Okay, Tovarich, *pana say Russki? Sprechen sie Deutsch?* Double Pronto!"

"What?" asked the bewildered Link.

"Come on, fella. Would you rather talk now, or spend a couple hundred years in jail?"

"I'll be happy to talk now, General."

"Oh, you would, would you?" The general sneered. "Who's putting you up to it?"

The Stearman Duster was gaining on the copter.

"Open her up, Omar!" cried Olympus.

The wobbling plane was making Wilson airsick.

"I don't feel so good, Jake!" he cried.

"Hang on! They're getting away!" cried Jake. The glow in his collar became intense as the makeshift plane picked up speed.

"Can't you just zap 'em?" cried Wilson.

"With Liz and Lucy Belle in there?" yelled

the cat. "It takes all my power just to keep this thing airborne!"

Olympus was beginning to sense this. He studied the plane with his binoculars. "They're in trouble," he said.

"I wouldn't trust them, sir," said Stallwood. "Not as long as they have that collar."

"Which they'll never use!" growled Olympus. "Not as long as we have the woman and her cat! If they destroy us, they'll have to destroy *them!* Not in a million years!" He reached a decision. "We *attack!*"

Omar glanced back. "What?" He was apprehensive.

"Attack, sir?" cried Stallwood, his voice cracking. "You don't really mean we . . ."

"We attack!" thundered Olympus.

Omar brought the copter up, then swooped down. Its blades cut off the tip of the Duster's wing.

"They're trying to kill us!" cried Wilson.

"Would appear so," said Jake. He took elusive measures. Now he was on the defensive.

Down came the copter and chopped off the Duster's tail.

"Jake!" screamed Wilson.

"I see it!"

Another pass from the copter. Their undercarriage was sliced away. It sailed off and split into sections.

The copter disappeared.

"Where is it? I don't see it!" cried Wilson. He peered in all directions.

"Here she comes, Frank! Duck!" cried Jake. From an overhead cloud bank, the copter bore down. Its skids now rested on the Stearman's top wing.

"They're on our wings! They're forcing us down!" cried Wilson.

Jake flew straight at a suspension bridge. The copter rose above the bridge and the Duster flew under it. It came back on the wing and Jake headed directly toward a huge lighter-than-air balloon. The pilot in the basket could be seen waving his arms and screaming. The copter flew over the balloon, the plane dropped under it.

"That does it!" cried Olympus. "Buzz them one more time, Omar! Everybody open fire!"

All but Stallwood withdrew weapons from their jackets. He had none to withdraw. He removed a large flare gun attached to the bulkhead.

Omar made the pass. They shot through the open doorway.

"Oh, ho!" grinned Stallwood. "This is fun, sir!" A burst from his flare gun. "Just like in the movies!" he cried excitedly.

The copter tailed off to avoid the Stearman's maneuver and Stallwood rolled back on the floor, accidentally shooting through the fuselage. It was ripped and smoking. The copter began to sputter, then cough.

"Are you out of your mind, Stallwood?" screamed Olympus.

"Wha—what happened?!" cried Stallwood.

"*You* happened, you clothhead! How bad is it, Omar?"

"He got the fuel line, sir! It won't fly long!"

"What do we do, bail out?"

"No choice!" cried Olympus. "Chutes, everybody!"

They slipped into chutes and rushed toward the doorway. The copter began to wobble.

"What about *her?*" Choirmaster nodded toward Elizabeth.

"Untie her!" Olympus ordered. Choirmaster complied. "She can fly the plane!"

"But I can't fly a plane!" Elizabeth cried.

"Then you have a problem!" Olympus sneered.

"What about me?" Stallwood's face was ashen. "I don't have a parachute!"

"You have an even bigger problem!" Olympus snarled. He signaled. Choirmaster and Omar leaped. Far below, their chutes opened.

As Olympus prepared to jump, Stallwood grabbed his legs.

"I don't want to die, sir!"

"Let go, you idiot!" screamed Olympus, who tried to struggle free, failed, and fell. Stallwood was hanging on to his harness straps as they tumbled over and over, spinning earthward, clutched to each other. Stallwood's wail, at first a crescendo, tailed off and was gone. Liz frantically tried to right the copter.

Wilson saw it all. "They've all bailed out! All but Liz!" he cried.

"My collar's weakening!" cried Jake.

"We've got to help her, Jake!" yelled Wilson.

Dozens of army vehicles stood by as General Stilton took charge back on the airfield. He was speaking directly to the President of the United States. By radio phone.

". . . Yes, Mister President. . . . Absolutely, Mister President . . . we're just waiting for them to land, sir, then we'll effect that order, Mister President. . . . Yes, sir . . . I *will*, sir!" said the general. He hung up. Link stood beside him.

"That was the *President?*" Link was in awe.

"Presidential directive. Your friend Jake is to be treated as a representative of a friendly power. With generous borrowing credit. In exchange for bases, of course."

Sergeant Duffy came running up. Excitedly, he pointed toward the sky.

"Look, sir! Chutes! They've bailed out!"

Link glanced up. "Holy mackerel! Who's flying the copter?"

Liz was. Or was trying to. She was as good at flying copters as she was at playing pool.

"Hang on!" cried Jake. He brought the Duster alongside the copter.

"Take it under the skids!" yelled Wilson.

"What're you going to do?"

"Take her under, Jake!"

The plane swept under the copter's skids and held steady. Wilson climbed up to the top wing, made several futile passes at one of the skids, then finally clung on. He called. "C'mon, Liz!"

She was shaking. "I can't do it, Frank!"

"You can do anything, baby! I'll help! That's it! Easy! Come on! You're gonna be fine! We're going to make it, Liz! We're going to make it!"

Cautiously, patiently, he moved her from skid to wing. Then, ever so slowly, from wing to the cockpit. They were home free. Safe.

Lucy Belle purred.

Jake nosed her. "You are one beautiful doll."

Several thousand feet below, in a pine tree, hanging in the shrouds of their parachutes, were Omar and Choirmaster. Above them, in the same towering pine, was Olympus, clutching Stallwood's trousers. Stallwood, above him, was desperately clinging to the chute, impaled on a limb.

"Don't just hang there! Get me out of this!" ordered Olympus.

"Count on it, sir!" cried Stallwood.

"Not with *that!*" Olympus cried. "What're you doing?"

Stallwood held up a penknife.

"I never travel without my Swiss army knife, sir!"

"You imbecile!" screamed Olympus. *"Don't you dare!"*

He had reason to panic. The tree limb overhung a thousand-foot drop and a boulder-strewn bottom. One mistake, one slight move, and it would be over. Sirens could be heard. The general's command car swept up in convoy, with no end of escorts. This time, he was taking no chances. Beside Stilton, in the rear, sat Link, a guest. Up front, bunched together, were the general's three aides.

Troops jumped from vehicles, weapons at the ready, as the general leaped from his sedan. He surveyed the situation—the cliff, the tree, and the men desperately hanging in the branches. Stilton slapped his crop against his thigh.

"How are you at tree climbing, Colonel?" he barked.

"Uh . . ." the colonel said. *"Captain!"*

"Ser---geant!" yelled the captain.

The sergeant was resigned. "Double pronto, sir?"

"I've a better suggestion, General," Link chirped in. "Why not use a simple chain saw?"

Stilton laughed heartily. A little too heartily. He was all charm now. "The Air Force could use your kind, Link! You're too big for garbage!"

Chapter Eleven

The august Victorian courtroom contained few people that morning, upon orders of the President. There was a bailiff, a court clerk, a court stenographer, and, at the front entrance, two guards. In the front row were Wilson, Elizabeth, Link, and Lucy Belle.

Jake sat alone on a leather chair placed directly in front of the judge's bench. The bailiff rose and everyone stood, including Jake.

"Hear ye, hear ye, hear ye, the United States District Court, the honorable Judge Alvin Horsham presiding!" bellowed the bailiff.

The judge moved swiftly to the bench and sat. Everyone followed his example. A portly, dignified man in his late fifties, the judge peered over his steel-rimmed glasses to survey his courtroom. The day was an auspicious one for him. After all, handpicked by the Attorney General. His eyes landed on the cat.

He addressed it solemnly. "You have made application for citizenship of the United States of America."

The cat meowed firmly.

"It is a signal honor which implies not only rights, but duties and obligations," the judge said. "Voting. Serving on juries. Bearing arms."

"Meow," said the cat.

"Who is sponsoring this applicant?" the judge asked.

Wilson, Link, and Elizabeth rose. She was holding Lucy Belle.

"I am, your honor," said Wilson.

"Does this cat have a name?" the judge asked.

"Jake, your honor."

With a gesture, the judge suggested they sit. They did. Horsham took upon himself the full dignity of the court.

"Please stand, Jake," he said.

The cat obliged.

"Repeat after me," said the judge. Jake placed one paw over his heart. His collar began to glow.

"I, Jake . . ." began the judge.

"I, Jake . . ." began Jake. The voice was soft, but distinct. The judge's staff was awed. Voice transference of some sort, but *definitely* a voice. Horsham gulped. But he had been briefed and he quickly regained his composure. The cat's collar was in full radiance. Almost imperceptibly, the judge began to float. Then rise.

"Pledge allegiance to the flag of the United States of America . . ." continued the judge.

"Pledge allegiance to the flag of the United States of America . . ." said the cat. The judge was three feet above his chair and moving higher.

"And to the Republic for which it stands . . ."

"And to the Republic for which it stands . . ."

No stopping him now, twelve feet above his bench. His arms extended.

"One nation—under God—indivisible . . ."

"One nation—under God—indivisible . . ."

Together. *"WITH LIBERTY—AND JUS-TICE—FOR ALL!"*

Judge Alvin Horsham soared like a glorious majestic eagle.